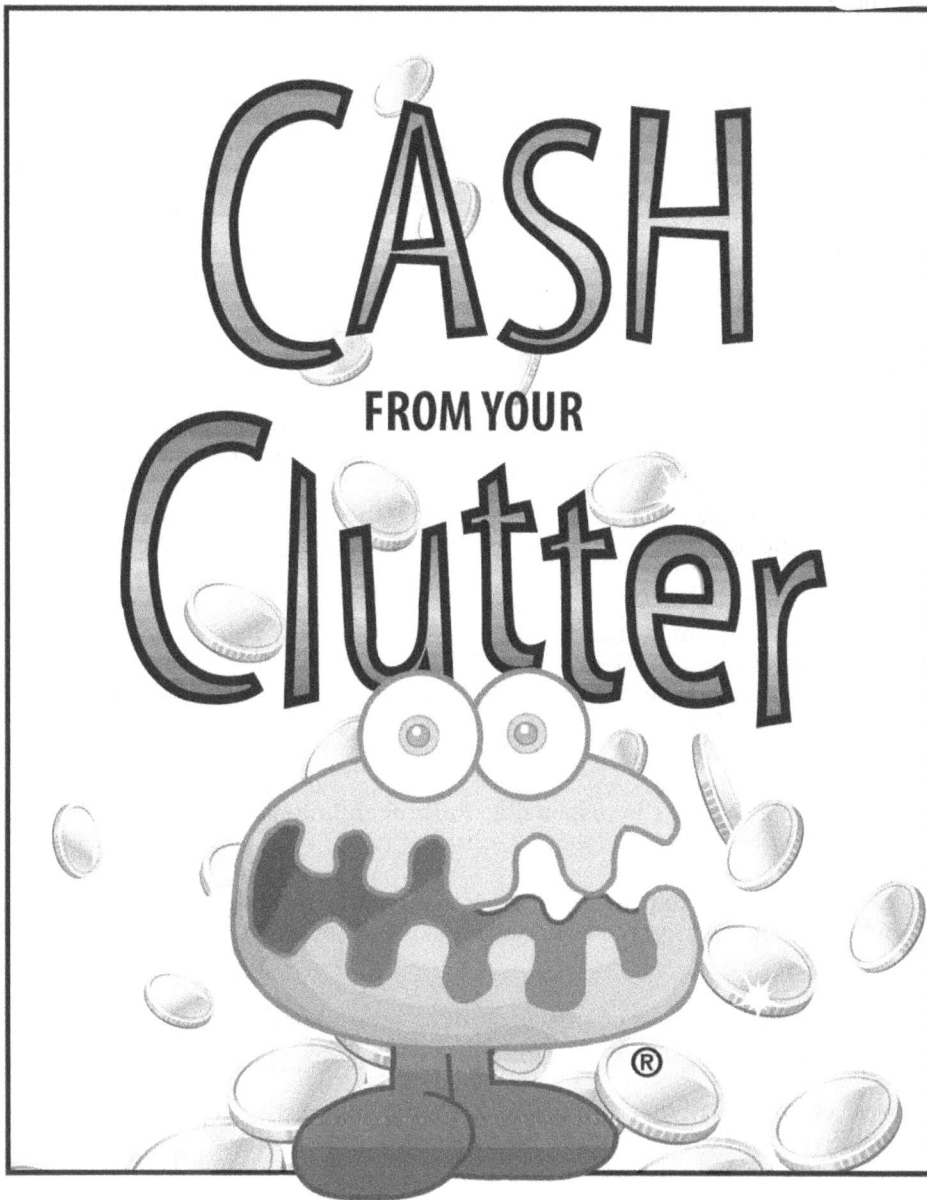

CASH

FROM YOUR

Clutter

NANCY MILLER

CPM Systems, Rancho Palos Verdes, California USA

CPM
SYSTEMS
PUBLISHING COMPANY
6318 Ridgepath Court
Rancho Palos Verdes, CA 90275-3248

CPMPub@RoundsMiller.com

The contents of this book are intended for information purposes only.

The information as described has been used successfully to obtain the results as advertised for some of the people who have used it. Although all efforts have been expended to supply the latest in complete, accurate and up-to-date information, it must be understood that the ultimate success of the user is dependent upon market conditions, efforts expended by the user, and other variable factors that are beyond the control of the author, and that neither the users' actual expenses nor successes are guaranteed nor implied.

At the time this edition was printed and released, all of the sites listed were active and accessible to anyone having access to the internet. Websites and information about service providers referred to in the publication have been researched and selected to provide relevant and up-to-date information on the subject matter as of the date of publication and every effort has been made to ensure that the information is correct at the time of publication.

Neither the author nor CPM Systems is responsible for broken links, abandoned sites, or changes that are beyond their control.

CPM Systems accepts no responsibility for the status, content, or functionality of any website referenced and does not endorse any specific products or services offered by any of the providers referenced in these sites.

Neither CPM Systems nor the author of this book offer any information in this book as a guarantee of performance, functionality, or outcomes.

Readers and users of this material are solely responsible for the research, verification, validation, application, operation and outcomes of any of the processes, organizations or services referenced.

Throughout this book, trademarked names are used. Rather than put a trademark symbol after every occurrence of the trademarked name, we used the names in an editorial fashion only, and to the benefit of the trademark owner, with no intention of infringement of the trademark.

This book is written with the understanding that the author is not engaged in rendering legal services. The information included has been carefully prepared and is correct to the best of their knowledge as of the publication date. If you require legal or expert advice, the services of professionals should be used. The author disclaims any personal liability, either directly or indirectly, for advice or information presented in this book.

This book contains excerpted copyrighted materials from Clutterology® Getting Rid of Clutter and Getting Organized.

First Printing, 2012
Printed in the United State of America
978-1-891440-73-1

ABOUT THE AUTHOR

Growing up, Nancy Miller was surrounded by garbage. Trash put food on the table. Her family owned the garbage service in Hutchinson, Minnesota; a small town that managed to create more refuse than one might imagine. No one knows clutter better than Nancy.

Like most Midwestern dreamers, she hopped a bus to Los Angeles, where she would work her way to the top. Now, all grown up, Nancy is an internationally-recognized expert on making space; helping people carve out the room they need to move, live, and create.

Over the past fifteen years, Nancy has achieved rock-star status in Personal Organizing circles. She sings her siren songs of simplicity and messages of minimalism to packed audiences (seated alphabetically in neat little rows) in over 150 performances each year. In 1997, Nancy was awarded the golden statue stars like her crave when she accepted "International Who's Who of Entrepreneurs" honors. (Following her own rule, when she brought the trophy home, she found something else to throw away or donate.)

She has earned numerous other awards, including the Golden Microphone Award for Speaking Excellence, awarded by the Greater Los Angeles Chapter of the National Speakers Association. She is also a past member of the National Association of Professional Organizers' Golden Circle. This elite designation recognizes Nancy's service in the War on Clutter and gives her a back-stage pass to professional development activities that will help her hone her craft, to secure her place in history as a decluttering legend.

Heralded as a modern-day Mary Poppins, Nancy wrote the books on getting organized, *Clutterology™ Getting Rid of Clutter and Getting Organized* and *The Clutter Bug Attacks Junk Mail, Spam and Telemarketers®*. During on-site consultations, Nancy collaborates with individuals, families, and businesses to ensure they have everything they need and want. And nothing they don't.

Neat woman. Neat ideas. Neat message.

If you are interested in additional books, CDs and videotapes, our website lists additional resources. For information on a consultation or speaking engagement with your group, please contact:

Nancy Miller, Clutterologist
6318 Ridgepath Court
Rancho Palos Verdes CA 90275-3248
310-544-9502
Nancy@Clutterology.com
www.Clutterology.com
http://clutterology.wordpress.com
www.facebook.com/Clutterology
www.linkedin.com/in/clutterology
http://twitter.com/Clutterology

Clutterology® Support
Nancy offers several different ways to help you after taking Nancy's class or reading Clutterology®.

Bring the Clutterologist to Your Organization
Nancy can bring her message on how to get organized to your organization in a 20 minute, 60 minute or multi-day format. If you have a conference, church group, retreat or business luncheon, contact her for available dates.

Clutterology® Blog
What are blogs all about? There is new information out there. If you would like to get information on a regular basis (weekly), check out the Clutterology® blog. Designed to update the information in this book, it provides new tips, tricks, motivation, ideas and things that would interest you. Share it with friends and family. Share it with that person you know who REALLY NEEDS TO GET ORGANIZED! http://Clutterology.wordpress.com

Clutter Bug on Facebook Fan Page
The Clutter Bug has a Facebook Fan Page www.facebook.com/Clutterology or Like Nancy on her Facebook.

LinkedIn
To stay professionally networked on LinkedIn and stay connected go to www.linkedin.com/in/Clutterology

Twitter
Need a little motivation on a weekly basis? Get weekly tweets from The Clutter Bug as she provides quick tips, ideas and updates for you. Tweet her on Twitter at http://twitter.com/Clutterology

Refer a Friend
Refer a friend who becomes a client or provide a lead for a paid speaking engagement or a free speaking engagement with product sales of more than $1,000.00 and Nancy will give you your choice of:

❏ One-hour of hands-on consulting
❏ Two-hours of telephone coaching
❏ A three-month topic specific group
❏ Clutter Reinforcement Class

Do You Have A Clutter Tip?
Send Nancy your clutter busting tip and we'll share it with others.

TABLE OF CONTENTS

ACKNOWLEDGEMENTS

To my husband, Mike, an incredible collector of information.

My thanks to all the librarians who helped with researching the books for this book. Who knew that you could max out your library card?

To all my clients who have expanded my horizons and accepted the challenge to reduce their collections.

Cash from YOUR CLUTTER

Chapter 1
Cash From Your Clutter

It seems that we spend the first half of our life collecting stuff and then we spend the second half of our life trying to getting rid of stuff. As a professional organizer, I have helped many individuals organize their homes. Often times, they didn't want to just toss the things they had, so from their experiences came the birth of *Cash From Your Clutter*.

What can we do with things other than toss them? Is it possible to make some money? How hard is it? Where do I go? Who do I ask? So where do I start?

There are many ways and it may depend on how the stuff arrived at your front door. Did you inherit it from a family member that has passed way? Or from several family members who have passed? Or was it the silent type of accumulation that slowly crept into your home while you weren't looking? Or are you the eccentric type—having had several hobbies, interests, likes, passions or careers in your past?

My dad was a collector, so I grew up going to horse auction on the first Sunday of the month. My dad, my brother and I went to the horse auction together. The first part of the day was the horse tack (saddles, bridles, blankets, brushes, etc.) and then the second half was the horses. I was always excited when Dad bid on something. We never came home with much but often came home with something (or things).

Dad also spent time at what are called farm auctions. This was when a farmer was selling items from the farm—sometime a few items from the house, sometimes it included farm equipment and tools.

My mother liked antiques, and had a couple of favorite items she collected. One was antique irons (flat irons) that were put onto the stove and heated up. When the iron got hot, then the clothes were pressed. I liked the one for pleats (a pleating iron). We used them around the house as door stops and book ends.

The other items that caught her eye were antique piano stools with eagle claw feet. Those were cool.

Dad was an entrepreneur. He purchased our hometown garbage business, which came with the local dump. My dad and brother had their own version of dumpster diving—the whole dump! They wandered the dump and picked up what they wanted. Dad had to purchase a building large enough to store the garbage trucks. That was a barn. Since there were only two garbage trucks, that left 3/4 of the barn for his stuff! And he worked at filling it up!

A small collection that my dad had was colored glass bottles. As a gentleman farmer (he had less than 18 acres), when he plowed the field, every once in a while, he uncovered an old bottle. He put it on a shelf in his office in the barn. He taught me about the age and manufacturing of bottles. I can pretty much tell when a bottle was mass produced or hand blown.

I'm not without my collecting hobby. It was the British Royal Family. I was a very good collector. Thank heavens for me; this was before the internet and eBay. I think we might be broke with everything that is available now. At the height of my collection, I had over 500 books and 3000 magazines, some dolls, and I spoke on the subject. The day before Diana's funeral, I was on the Leeza Show on a panel with Pierra Salinger. Then one day, I realized that I had become obsessive compulsive. I called a buyer, and sold the lot. And that was the end of my collection.

WHERE TO START

The concept of this book is that there are things lying around your home that could bring you money. Some things may be obvious, like piles that you have set aside for a garage sale someday. Things you may have inherited, but you and your other family members don't want them.

You have closets full of perfectly good things; some with price tags still on them. You may be crafty; you've made things that you could sell. So start looking through those drawers, closets, attics, garages and storage units for items that could bring in money. I'll also toss in a couple of items that are just plain silly.

When I started this project, a friend of ours gave us two great examples of money that was sitting around his house.

Several years ago, Hector went to a big box store to get an estimate for a repair on his house. For them to come out to his house and take the exact measurements to get the project rolling, all that was required now, was a deposit. He gave them the deposit and an appointment was scheduled. Then rescheduled, and rescheduled.

Time passed, months went by, and five years have come and gone. The project that the deposit secured has not happened. So Hector went to the store and inquired about getting his deposit back. Everything was on their computer. No, they weren't able to refund the deposit but were able to provide store credit.

Another example, Hector was having guests to his home so he thought an airbed was a great solution. Unable to decide in the store between two different inflatable mattress designs, he decided to purchase both, make the final decision at home and return the unselected design.

Time passed, the receipt was lost, neither airbed was every used! Eventually Hector decided to take them both back. The big department store would not provide a credit to his credit card but they provided store credit.

As in both of these examples of store merchandise, go back to the store to inquire and see what they can do (with or without a receipt). Some stores will, some won't, some can, some can't, on some days they will, on some days they won't. But if you don't ask, you won't know.

Let's get started in your house with a pile or section of the house. This may be the garage, junk room, attic, or someplace where all the stuff just seems to collect. For some, this could be a storage unit.

Start by going through your home to collect the items that you'd like to sell. In my book, Clutterology® Getting Rid of Clutter and Getting Organized, I talk about what's known as the four-box system. I have modified it for this book.

There are only four things that you can do with any item. So as you start to clean out your space, get four boxes to put stuff in. Sort as follows:

1. Toss it. These items will go in the trash. Use a black trash bag so once the item is in the *toss* box, you don't see it again (and start missing it).

2. Fix it. These items need to be taken care of or fixed. The first time you do this sorting exercise, I recommend that you take the items in this box and donate them. There are times when a little bit of fixing up will bring more money, but we don't want you to over complicate the system early-on.

3. Sell it. (Hey this is what *Cash From You Clutter* is all about!)

4. Give it. Find a good home for the things that you no longer use that still have life left in them. Friends, charity (more on this later in the book on page 45) or recycling are all wonderful options.

After you're finished sorting, all the remaining un-boxed items are things you have elected to keep. This should be a very small portion of your stuff.

SHOW ME THE MONEY

Old doesn't always mean gold

This is a quote from one of the television shows. As you are going through your stuff, don't keep an item just because it's old; and just because it's old, don't expect that you're going to get rich. Don't expect your things to bring a lot of money—like on television. It may take a lot more time than you may think.

Rule of thumb 20/50/30

Twenty percent will sell right away

Fifty percent will take a little longer

Thirty percent will be difficult to sell

If you watch some of the television shows, there are people called pickers. A picker is a person that gathers or collects. They go to swap meets, garage sales, flea markets and they knock on people's doors to *discover* hidden gems. They buy at wholesale prices and they only pick a few items. Even when they have a big truck that they can fill, they only pick a few items. They are looking for the cream. So in your collection, as much as you would like a white knight to come in and buy everything, it probably will be one person that buys just a few items.

How to place a realistic value on your stuff:

1. What you paid.

2. What you can get.

3. What you need.

4. What you'll take.

So how are you going to determine the value of an item (or at least a ballpark figure)?

First go to eBay and do a search. Check out: is the item being offered, how many are being offered, what the price range is, and what past sales have been. Unlike playing horseshoes, *close* doesn't count. The condition, the year, and the packaging are very big factors in determining the value of the product. The BIG difference here is look for the **SOLD** price not the price being offered. Any price can be offered.

Second, check the price book to see the published the prices. Has there been a recent auction catalog? If a similar item has been sold at a recent auction, you can do a comparison valuation.

Here is a tip for your emotions: the dollar figures in these books are just prices—don't think it is the price that someone will pay if they are buying it from you. They want to BUY it at half that figure or less. Don't get excited, don't thing that you are going to get rich. You may be only able to sell one piece at the book value, not everything, and not all at once. Go back and read the rule of thumb.

Third, go to the library and research books on the subject of your collection. Also consider bookstores and Amazon.com to purchase books (caution: save your money). At the bookstores, visit the magazine racks and get subject specific magazines (antiques, bicycling, dolls, and toys) and perhaps purchase an issue.

The books that have the price guides are typically Warman's, Kovels' and Schroeder's.

You may want to check out the association or society for your collection. They have shows, events, newsletters, evaluations, and other information that may help you to evaluate your collection.

Fourth, start to visit flea markets, swap meets, and indoor antique malls. Pick up magazines, flyers, and newspapers and look over the ads and become familiar with the upcoming shows, events, names of experts, etc. Go to the show (maybe) to sell your items, or for appraisals, etc.

Fifth, take a few of your best items in to get an appraisal. An appraisal may cost so watch for free appraisals. Check with your local library and auction houses in your area as they may offer a free service either monthly or once a year (see the above paragraph for resources).

The type of appraisal you want is a **fair market value**. An appraisal will cost you either by the hour ($100 to $300 per hour) or per item.

Do you have items that you have an insurance appraisal (value) for? You're saying, oh this will be easy; I'll just sell for that. Nope. About 20 percent of that. I don't know why and I don't understand it, but their appraisal insurance value, and what people will pay for that item, are very, very different numbers.

Check to see that the appraiser is a certified appraiser or ask the appraiser about USPAP (Uniform Standards of Professional Appraisal Practice). If the appraiser doesn't know about USPAP, you may want to consider another individual. Their legal documents will be for insurance, tax or other purposes.

Books:
Price It Yourself! Joe L. Rosson 0-06-009684-5 Chapter 3 Getting to Know All About It: The Appraisal Process and Chapter 4 Reality Check Factors That Add and Subtract Value.

Sell, Keep or Toss? Harry L. Rinker 978-0-375-72240-0 Chapter 1 What are My Things Worth [he makes good points] decorative, reuse, valuable, antique, book value. He also addresses scrap metals.

HOW OLD IS AN ANTIQUE?

Age, age, age—it is all relative! Or is it?

So what are we talking about? What is an antique? Growing up in Minnesota, I had a very good idea of what an antique was. When I moved to California, that definition seemed to have changed! The definition also changes when you move into different categories. Think Disney (Disneyana) which is just approaching 100 years. Within that category they have antique and vintage.

Antique: An antique is an object that is at least 100 years old and is rare and unique. Made totally by a person (hand-made) is often relevant.

Vintage: A vintage item can be from virtually any decade or era. A 100 year old couch, for example, could be described as antique furniture. An Art Deco couch from the 1930s would be considered vintage. Even when surviving for 100 years, the Art Deco couch could still be described as vintage because of its specific design.

Collectible: A collectible is an item that was made by machine.

Merchandising: Merchandising is the promotion of goods. Think about recent years where a sport fan picks up all the merchandise at the World Series of that beloved team in the play off. Although the item does fall into a collectible category (produced by a machine), the team promoted the products more than the world in general was collecting the items. For example, I had a whole lot of Charles and Diana merchandise in my collection.

Isn't New But Not Old AKA Rock and Hard Place: The problem many have is that their items are neither antique nor collectible. They are just recent things from around the house that are no longer needed that you would like to get rid of. The pricing books won't be of much help because your item is considered far too new. The dealers aren't interested because the item hasn't aged enough. When you take the item to a consignment store, the item is too old; they want little newer items. Your spouse wants the item out of the house because it has aged more than enough. Is this the definition of a rock and a hard place?

I've done my best to give you a variety of different methods and resources to help you cash in your stash of stuff, making your available home and office space more accessible, while inflating your bank account.

Here is what I am assuming about your stuff. You have a household full of it, or a collection of it, you inherited it. The bottom line is, you want or need to get rid of it. Don't get so wrapped up in this project, so good at it, that you want it to become a business for you!

There are two types of styles for selling your stuff.

- Do you want someone else do it for you?

- Do you want to do it yourself?

When you allow someone else to do it for you, it'll typically be on consignment or put into an auction house or an estate sale. If you feel this suits your style, jump straight over to Chapter 2.

Doing it all yourself could mean be a garage sale (and all the similar types of yard sales, etc.) or selling the item online. I'll cover this in detail in Chapter 3.

If you have a collection of items, Chapter 4 is where you'll want to turn.

You are probably overwhelmed to begin with so to simplify your resources, here is the process.

There is a quick **definition or explanation of the product or category,** then a list of up to three **storefronts** [brick and mortar stores] with multiple national-locations so you can take your stuff there. When multiple national-locations storefronts were not available, I then recommended the best single resource I could find.

Then I've provided a list of up to three **online sources** where you can sell your stuff.

I've provided a **book** (or books) for you to reference and learn more. The book(s) should be available at your local library, so you don't have to spend money since the idea is to make money. If you find that the book is very good, then you may want to purchase it.

I tried to find books that would value the item. There were only a few of them. Many of the books were selected for only a page or two as they explain how to care, repair or restore a particular collectible. Or the book may have an excellent (compared to other similar books) reference section in the back of the book.

Cash From Your Clutter covers many topics and subjects including garage sales, auctions, collections, etc. Each individual topic has books written about them. More information is available at your local library by exploring the book shelves, talking with the reference librarian and become an expert yourself on the areas you need to know.

Suggestions for where (and to whom) you can **donate** specific items are in Chapter 4; both a storefront [brick and mortar store] with multiple national-locations, and then a place where you could ship the item if you would like. The only reason I would suggest that you incur this additional expense is because of the uniqueness of the item or the charity.

There are so many television shows that I wanted to make reference to them on occasion. For visual people, sometimes, watching a program is easier than reading a book. Television is for entertainment. Your reality may be very different!!

You are probably excited about selling all this stuff and making big bucks because you caught a couple of television shows like American Pickers, Cash Cowboy, Picked Off, Pawn Stars, Antiques Roadshow, What The Sell?!, or Hoarder (oops, that's my other book) and you saw that one item where you have the exact same thing, or one that is really, really close, that sold for mega bucks. Well, television is entertainment. You probably won't make that kind of money.

I have referenced television shows as you may learn something when you watch them, as part of your research. Don't expect your results to be the same either in time, money or effort.

Chapter 5 will **wrap it up** with any additional comments for that item. Where you can donate your items that you can't sell, smaller charities that are looking for specific items, and how to document your charitable donation for your tax records.

What I don't want you to do is to make this an ongoing business. At some point, this project will come to an end. That's when we wrap it up with Chapter 5.

This book and the processes involved will help you look at your clutter in a whole new way so that rather than wanting to hold onto it, for whatever the reason, you'll be anxious to trade it for ready cash so that you can get some new things.

Book:
How to Make a Fortune With Other People's Junk G.G. Carbone 0-07-144642-7. Chapter 11 Understanding Trends and Establishing Value will help you to figure out how much your stuff may be worth with internet searches, eBay searches, library's resources, price guides, tends and fads, etc. Chapter 12 Selling Your Treasures Through the Experts has some words of wisdom also. Nice resource section wit antique shows, flea markets, magazines/journals and newspapers.

Letting Someone Else

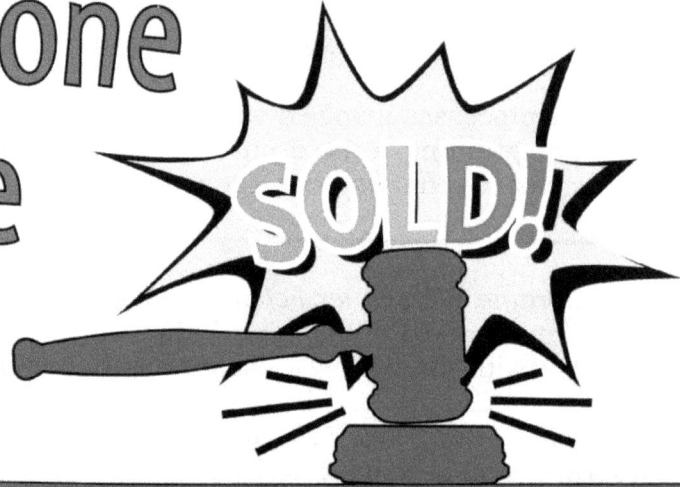

SOLD!

SELL YOUR STUFF

Chapter 2
Letting Someone Else Sell Your Stuff!

There are so many places where you could sell your things—stores (brick and mortar), whether they are small *mom and pops* store or the big box stores, and online: including big auction locations or specialty websites. There are places to sell almost all general items. Let's take a look at where you can hand over your stuff to someone to sell your *everythings* and *anythings*. These stores are in alphabetical order for your convenience.

AUCTION HOUSES

If you have a valuable item that you feel warrants an auction house, there are several things you can do.

You've heard the names before, Christie's or Sotheby's, or the local hometown auctioneer. Each auction house has different criteria. The criteria may be based on a dollar figure or on an area of works. Often times, they can provide a referral to another firm or appraisal.

1. Contact the International Society of Appraisers www.isa-appraisers.org 888-472-4732, or the American Society of Appraiser www.appraisers.org 800-272-8258, and talk with them. They may be able to refer you to a local contact or a specialist.

   There is a LinkedIn Group: American Society of Appraisers join or comment on the discussion.

2. Contact the auction house and inquire about a public appraisal day. Take an item or two that you feel is valuable and have it appraised. Based on the value, decide what to do next.

3. If you have a lot of items of obvious value, the auction house may send a representative out for a site appraisal.

4. Auction estimate: an auction house will give you an estimate of what your item may sell for were you to use their services. The estimate is usually free and limited to a few items.

Pros:
- They deal in rare or high-end or medium range items.

- This is their business.

- They advertise the sale.

- You turn it over to them and they do everything for you.

- Your will be paid within 7-35 days.

Cons:

- The sale isn't going to be tomorrow, it may be in six months (or longer).

- There are fees such as handling, service charges, online catalog, illustration, insurance. It may seem like they are nickel and diming you to death.

- Their fee is a percentage of the selling price, ranging from 10 to 35 percent.

- Broker fees: either a flat fee or a commission

Sotheby's Appraisal Department 212-606-7000 www.sothebys.com

International Society of Appraisers 888-472-4732

Christie's 310-385-2600 www.Christies.com

Bonham's International Auctioneers 323-857-5600

Virtual Auction Houses:
eBay www.eBay.com

iCollector.com 866-313-0123 www.icollector.com

National Auctioneers Association 931-541-8048 www.auctioneers.org

Check your local city (chamber of commerce or city hall as they may have contact information) for a local auction house.

Go to AuctionZip 814-623-5059 www.Auctionzip.com to find auction houses that are located near you.

Television Show:
Auction King, Paul Brown, 2010 to present, 30 minutes Discovery Channel. They usually follow three items from coming into the auction house through the end of the auction. This is a good program to watch when you're planning to put items up for auction.

Book:
Buy, Keep or Sell? Judith Miller 0-7566-1338-8. This has a good reference section. It also has clubs and societies. There is information on auction houses.

CONSIGNMENT STORE

A consignment store is a second-hand store where you can sell (consign) your clothes. Call to make an appointment first. Then take your clothes in, the store will select the clothes that they want to take on consignment. There will be a specific time frame—30 days, 60 days, etc. Then you have to come back and pick up unsold items. If the merchandise is sold, the owner of the store splits the profit with you. The split may vary from 40 percent to 60 percent. Prices/pricing varies depending upon item, demand and location.

The stores are very selective (very current [1-2 year fashion window] and seasonal) about what they choose. Spend some time on the phone and find a consignment store that has the type of clothes you want to put on consignment. The consignment store may not be *open* (accepting) for new clients at this time, or the store may be a children's store and only wants children's clothes.

Clothes must be clean, in excellent condition and usually on hangers. (Different stores may have a slight variation on this).

You will be asked to sign a consignment contract. Be sure you understand it.

The consignment categories that generally products fall into are:

1. Children's clothing

2. Children's toys

3. Furniture

4. Home furnishings

5. Jewelry

6. Men's clothing

7. Women's clothing

Pros:
- You don't have to set the price.

- You don't have to deal with the public.

- You don't have to advertise.

Cons:
- You have to wait to get paid (when they sell it).

- They are seasonal. You can't bring in winter clothes in June.

- The stores are picky.

- The clothes have to be clean and possibly on hangers.

- Not everything sells.

- http://howtoconsign.com/find.htm This is a website that will locate consignment stores in your state.

- Associations, Societies and LinkedIn Groups:

- Consignment and Resale currently has over a 1,000 members. You may wish to join.

- The National Association of Resale Professionals 800-544-0751 www.NARTS.org

You won't want to miss this one.

ANOTHER AUCTION BY FAHEY

FORD TRACTOR AND EQUIPMENT - ANTIQUES - WOODWORKING TOOLS - LOTS OF LUMBER AND WOOD

 # AUCTION

Located at 185 Arch Street SE, Hutchinson, MN. Take 2nd Avenue east from Adams Street (Hwy 22). Cross r first farm on left.

TUESDAY, OCTOBER 21, 1997   2:00 PM

Be on time.   Many items!   Lunch and restroom on grou

FORD TRACTOR, 3 PT. AND FARM EQUIPMENT, FARM MISCELLANEOUS

Ford 2000 gas with wide front, 3 pt., front pump and fenders (blue) with Deereborn full hyd. loader, sells as unit, looks and runs good.

Attachments separate: 3 pt. weight box; front bumper; Ford jack, 12.4x28 chains. Sweco 6 ft. 3 pt. V snowblower; Deereborn 3 pt. sickle mower; Deereborn 3 pt. 6 ft. adjustable blade; Howse 5 ft. 3 pt. rotary cutter; McCormick 2-wheel ground drive spreader; salvage 2-wheel trailer; homemade double horse trailer; CharLynn pump; platform scale; Jari-type sickle mower; garden tools; asst. tarps; small 6'x8' wooden corn crib (old); asst. cable; steel and wood fence posts; some timbers; 55 gal. barrels; some scrap iron; 4"x18' electric auger; asst. cages; log chains; 2 wheel lawn cart; Here

ANTIQUES

8 ft. oak display case with glass top and sides (very good condition); several old trunks; 4-door glass cupboard top; large library table; 4-door wainscoted cupboard; old paper roll holder; birdhouses (old); old 2-seated glider swing; milk cans and cart; potato plow; walking cult; asst. old oil bottles and cans; wash stomper; asst. round stove pipe gra horse hames; dry wall sink cupboard; old cafe cabinet; double pedestal w desk; lots of misc. small antique items; cast iron bath tub with feet; small w stove;

WOODWORKING, POWER & HAND TOOLS

Power Craft band saw; B&D power mitre saw; Craftsman 6x48 belt sander \ stand; Wood Master #1200 12" drum sander on base; 4" jointer on stand; elec hack saw; Sears 101 48" wood lathe on stand; Mac chain saw; Forney welder; of hand tools and power tools; lots of C clamps and wood clamps; 2 grinders stands; electric motors; rollers and stands; 2-wheel H.D. cart; 2 sections p rack; H.D. floor jack; 2 sump pumps; tool boxes; screw jacks; lots of hardw large asst. of cabinet hardware;

CRAFT LUMBER AND WOOD

HUGE selection, literally tons, of craft lumber, mostly pine and maple; some hardwood chair parts; all sizes of table legs; chair bases; roll-top desk ends; cabinet doors (some panelled); 19"x50" oak pcs.; 10"x42" oak pcs.; asst home-sawed white, red and green

My family's farm auction

Book:
The Ultimate Consignment & Thrift Store Guide Carolyn Schneider 0-9656571-1-6. This book gives a list of consignment stores and their preferred items.

ESTATE SALES

Generally estate sales are held Wednesday through Saturday (Saturday being a half-price day). They can be by appointment only when they are in restricted sales areas.

An estate sale is more extensive than a garage sale. As the name implies, it's usually the liquidation of an entire single-family estate (all the contents of a home) and it's most often conducted by a professional service or agent, for a fee. An estate sale is often held when a property owner has passed away and their belongings need to be liquidated. Estates sales also occur after a divorce when the couple is dividing the assets. Another example could be that someone is moving and downsizing in a major way. My husband recalls an estate sale that was a garage sale in the city of Rolling Hills ESTATES.

Pros:
• Estate sales are usually conducted by a professional estate sales person.

• They may have a mailing list of people, buyers and collectors.

• They set up, advertise the sale, manage the sale and clean up afterwards.

• Estate sales are more organized than a garage sale.

• Items are cleaned, classified and organized.

• An expert sets the price.

• An estate sale last 2-3 days.

• Merchandise that moves fast are personal items such as shampoo.

Cons:
• Setting up an estate sale take many hours, depending on the volume of the merchandise.

• The service may take 10 to 30 percent of gross sales, or a flat fee.

• There is a dumpster charge to remove the trash.

Some questions to ask when interviewing for an estate agent:
• How do you advertise?

• How do you handle the crowd?

• How does staff oversee closed areas of the house (off limit areas)?

• How (what) do you clean up after the sale?

Estate Sales Network www.EstateSales.net Finds estate sales, a tag sale, or an Auction.

Average figures at an Estate Tag Sale:
About 30 percent of everything marked with too low a price will be sold.

About 50 percent will be sold at discounted prices.

About 20 percent will need to be disposed of or given away.

0 percent will be sold for more than it is marked.

Tag sales are negative negotiation sales methods where the price can only go down, not up.

Books:
Treasures In Your Attic Joe L. Rosson 0-06-019927-3. This is a good book up to a point. It is good for a quick read and will give you a quick and good education on your things. It will even give you an idea how much the stuff might be worth (example: men's neck ties). It doesn't give you any idea where to get rid of your stuff. The Third Section Professional Advice covers estate sales and finding an appraiser.

Have Sale – Will Travel Betty DeKlyne 0-9651559-0-0. This is a cute and useful book. It is written for people planning on become an estate sale agent. The information is very good even when you are just planning to have an estate sale. There is a chapter of what the agent shouldn't do to you and a chapter on what you shouldn't do to the agent. If you are planning an estate sale, this is a good book to read as a primer.

BIG BOX STORES

You drive by them every day and have probably purchased some of your electronics from them. Some of these companies are now making it easy for you to trade-in older goods. Some offer sell back program or may buy back old electronics.

Technology changes quickly, so as soon as you upgrade, sell your old technology. Don't wait! By waiting too long, you may get very little or nothing for the electronics. When you do have old or older electronics lying around the house, at least attempt to use these sources, you never know. As the old saying goes, "If you don't ask, you don't get!"

Pros:
- If you sign up for a buyback program when you first buy the equipment you don't have to think out what to do when you upgrade.

- These stores are extremely convenient.

- You don't have to ship your electronics.

- You don't have to negotiate a deal.

Cons:
- If you have signed up for a buyback program, they may not give you the best price.

- You have no idea how long these programs will be in place (available).

Best Buy 888-237-8289 www.bestbuytradein.com

Target 888-969-4763 http://target.nextworth.com/

Wal-MartTradeIn 800-351-6864 http://walmart.cexchange.com/online/home/index.rails

Websites:

Since there are so many websites devoted to buying, selling, trading of the latest (or not so latest) electronics, here are several websites for you to check out and decide for yourself.

Here are a few things to check first:
- Check with the Better Business Bureau for reviews and ratings. It's always good to check. In the past couple of years, the BBB is not the consumer watch-dog it used to be.

- Do they provide a mailing label and/or prepaid box?

- When do you get payment (received within 10 days)?

- How do they handle personal information (such as information on your hard drive or your SIM card)?

  Some cell phones contain a portable Subscriber Identity Module (SIM) card that saves all of your personal information such as phone numbers, contacts and text messages. When upgrading you may wish to remove the SIM card (it will look like a small computer chip). Shred the card using scissors to damage the bronze foil area of the chip where the data is stored as thoroughly as possible and throw away the pieces.

Typical electronics are:
- smart phones (including Android, Blackberry, iPhone and Windows phone 7 devices)

- iPods

- tablets

- video games

Vendors:
Game Stop 303-955-5554 www.gamestop.com/trade

Next Worth 888-969-4763 www.NextWorth.com

Retrevo Inc 855-738-7386 www.Retrevo.com

PAWN SHOPS

A pawn shop is where a person can get a short term loan (up to 120 days) that is collateralized with property. When a person retrieves an item *out of pawn*, they are repaying the loan plus the interest within that stated period of time. Items not retrieved in a stated time period are sold.

We are looking at the other side of the pawn shop where the pawn shop buys merchandise. As they will be re-selling the item, their offer may be 50 percent or less of the value of item.

Pros:
- You get your money immediately.

- They tend to take a variety of items.

- You don't have to do any work.

- They pay in cash.

Cons:
- They offer you wholesale prices, not retail.

- Sometimes they don't have the customers for your unique item.

National Pawn Brokers Association 817-337-8830 www.nationalpawnbrokers.org

Television Show:
Pawn Stars, Richard (Old Man) Harrison, Rick Harrison, Corey (Big Hoss) Harrison, and Austin (Chumlee) Russell, 2009 to present, History Channel, 30 minutes. We have become a fan of this show and seem to always learn something. They mix in a few business lessons (make Rick money), such as valuing items and negotiating with individuals. The end of the show often ends with *the boys* shooting an antique firearm of some kind!

Cajun Pawn Stars, Jimmie DeRamus, 2012 to present, History Channel, 30 minutes. Jimmie knows everyone (it's a hometown, small town), he even pawns animals. Based in Louisiana, there are more new guns, Confederate memorabilia, and music legends here.

Hardcore Pawn, Les Gold, Seth Gold, Ashley (Gold) Broad, 2009 to present, truTV Channel, 30 minutes. It's amazing how two different networks can approach the same subject differently. Based in Detroit, this show focuses more on the pawning and problems (someone bought a vehicle and the two days later came back to the store, argued with the staff, had to be physically removed from the store because of the escalation of argument claiming the vehicle was defective only to find out it had run out of gas. The inventory and size of the pawn shop is huge.

Selling YOUR STUFF

Chapter 3
Selling Your Stuff

So you have decided to do it yourself, but what are you actually going to do or have? Is it a yard sale or a garage sale? Martha Stewart talks about a tag sale? What is involved in the sale: identifying salable pieces, prices, cleaning, arranging, advertising, security, and disposes of unsalable items. So, let's define what's what—in alphabetical order.

BOOT SALE

- English swap meet, where they sell from the back (boot) of their car!

- Items are usually previously owned.

- Usually held during the summer.

- Held at school grounds, grass fields, etc. on the weekend.

MOVING SALE

- Implies that the sellers are getting rid of stuff so they don't have to move it.

- It's not just *spring cleaning*.

RUMMAGE SALE

- Refers to the digging out treasure at a garage sale.

- People went to a rummage sale to search (rummage) through the stuff.

- It is used to mean a garage sale.

Book:
Rummage, Tag & Garage Sales Irma & R.A. Pohl 978-0385195058. Good for both rummage and tag sales.

STREET FAIR

- Mostly new items are offered.

- Some prices can be negotiated.

- Held in a public place, on a street or a public parking lot.

> Book:
> *Handmade For Profit!* Barbara Brabec 0-87131-995-0. This book is good for how to design and layout a booth to maximize sales. There is also a craft fair reference guide in the back. If you plan to show your wares in a shopping center (mall), this book is good.

SWAP MEET

- Both new and second hand items are offered.

- Second hand items are usually for barter or trade-in.

- A public market place.

TAG SALE

- There is a price (tag) on each item.

- Sometimes the tags are priced with the amount (25¢) or a color (green for 25¢).

- The second and third day of the tag sale, the price is frequently discounted.

- Second hand items are sold at a discounted price.

- Discounted prices are not haggled for.

- These are more often found on the East Coast.

YARD SALE

- A yard sale is usually, but not always, the same thing as a garage sale.

- When people don't have a garage, they use their yard.

- Often a group of people participate together in this sale.

Items that sells well:
- Baby items

- Bicycles

- Clothing

- Furniture

- Lawn mowers

- Power tools

- Sports equipment

Book:
Garage and Yard Sales Pocket Idiot's Guide Cathy Pedigo 978-1592570829. This is a very good little book. It guides you through everything. What is good to sell at a garage/yard sale and what is not (hint: good things are cosmetics and hair products and bad things are antiques and hazardous products). It goes room by room to give you ideas of what else you could include in the sale, how to plan the sale (including the best time to have the sale); plus a whole chapter on advertising (including sample ads). Then there is a chapter for after the sale.

CO-OP/ANTIQUE MALL

You have walked into a shopping center and there is a store with antiques. As you walk up and down the aisles selecting a few items, you take them to a cashier to pay. Each little area is a different vendor that rents the space.

Why would you use them? An antique mall or co-op would be used when you had a whole lot of stuff to sell and you wanted to set up a display for a while. You don't want to make this a full time business. Antique malls or a co-op would be good for a short time option.

Pros
• You don't have to man the booth.

• You don't have to collect the money.

• You don't have to deal with the public.

Cons
• You don't get to interact with the public. If you are good at pitching your wares, your sales won't be as high as if you were there personally.

• You need to refresh your merchandise or turn-over your inventory.

• You may need to put some hours in at the Co-Op.

• The space is often small.

• If someone offers a lower price and the Mall calls and you are not available, the sale may be lost!

Books:
Crafts Market Place Argie Manolis 978-1558704336. This has a listing of shows, craft malls and much much more.

How to Show & Sell Your Crafts Kathryn Caputo 978-1558704473. This is a good book when you are setting up any type of a display (garage sale, street fair, mall show, etc.) as it shows how to set up a booth (height, depth) indoor and outdoor, and even what to exactly say to people. You are getting rid of what you have, not getting excited about this and accidently creating a business!

CRAFT SHOW

A craft show or fair is an event anywhere from a few up to hundreds of people is exhibiting their products. Often times using tables or more elaborate display booths. Most frequently held on the weekend. Craft shows are held both indoors and outdoors.

http://classifieds.excite.com in search engine type "crafts fair" for current listings.

Books:
The Basic Guide to Selling Arts & Craft James Dillehay 978-0962992308. This book has a good resource section which includes organizations, buyer's directories, craft fair guides and magazines and newsletters.

Crafting As a Business Wendy W. Rosen 0-8019-8632-X. This book has a Yellow pages section (yes, on yellow pages).

FLEA MARKETS

- Usually featuring local products; held annually, quarterly, monthly, weekly or daily.

- Products are sold *as is*.

- New merchandise as well as plants and food can be found at flea markets.

- It may be indoor or outdoor.

- The prices can be bartered.

- The sellers rent the table or space.

- Drive-in theatres are a popular location.

Book:
Antiquing for Dummies Ron Zoglin 0-7645-5108-6. There is only one section that is worth reading and that is Chapter 21: Selling Your Antiques. You may be able to gleam useful information where to sell your antiques.

GARAGE SALE

- Items are sold from their garage and driveway.

- Items are not well organized and placed in bulk on a table, on a blanket, or on the floor.

- Anyone can administer the sale.

- Items are often sold at a cheaper price than marked.

- The items are *pre-loved*.

- Customer can haggle for the price.

- The more items that you have, the better the sale.

- People expect bargains and cheap items.

Book:
Garage Sale Mania! Chris Harold Stevenson 978-155-870-106-9. This book is good for garage sales, yard sales or tag sales.

So now that you know what the differences are, you're ready for your sale!!

EBAY

Since it began in 1995, eBay has transformed, changed and evolved. It has made it for easy for people to clean out their closets. It has made it easy for collectors internationally to fill-in the gaps of their collection.

For me, I use eBay always as a default. Most of the time, the option is rather than throw it away, I sell it on eBay. Do I make money? Often times not really. Had I invested more time and researched on other online auctions, worked harder on the description, etc. I might have made more money. For me, I tend to be lazy. It is always my knee-jerk answer to testing many things. Try it!

Here is a neat tip. When you upgrade your phone and they are offering a two for the price of one grab it. But wait, you say, I don't need two phones. Great I say. Now, go to eBay and sell that second phone that you just got.

You just purchased a state-of-the-art phone for zero money. Offer it on eBay for something more than that (100 percent, 50 percent, and 25 percent). Don't wait or put the new phone down, getting around to it in a month, because then the phone might not be worth anything! Right now, the sale of that second free phone is pure profit for you!

Here is another great way to use eBay. Do you have something that is broken around the house? Sell it for parts on eBay. There are people that have the exact same thing and still want to keep it. So they buy your things just for the parts!

Here are some definitions of what these words mean. These are helpful when you are looking at your items, especially with online auctions.

New: A brand-new, unused, unopened item in its original packaging, with all original packaging materials included. Original protective wrapping, if any, is intact. Original manufacturer's warranty, if any, still applies, with warranty details included in the listing comments.

New with tags: very desirable on online auctions.

Like new: an apparently untouched product, in perfect condition.

Very good: a well-cared-for product that has seen limited use but remains in great condition.

Good: The product shows wears from consistent use, but remains in good condition.

Acceptable: The item is fairly worn but continues to work perfectly. Signs of wear can include aesthetic issues such as scratches, dents, and worn corners. The item may have identifying markings on it or show other signs of previous use.

Non-functioning: these include products that require repair or service.

Pros:
*   You can sell items fast.

*   It's a great way to get rid of stuff.

*   You are paid for the item immediately.

*   Buyers from around the world bid on eBay.

Cons:
*   You probably won't make top dollar for the item.

*   Not all items sell—or won't sell the first time.

*   You need to ship the item.

*   People may ask questions—dumb questions or questions beyond your knowledge.

*   After you ship the item, the buyer may claim the item was damaged.

*   eBay is constantly changing their fee schedule.

CRAIGSLIST

Many people like Craigslist better than eBay because it's free. EBay has more buyers, better layout, and the pictures are in color.

Pros:
*   If you want to sell locally you don't have to ship.

*   Furniture, baby gear, power tools, and sports equipment may do well.

Cons:
*   Sellers don't use any or few photographs.

*   If you have a unique item, staying local may limit you too much.

In recent years, there have been several apps that have popped up and are quite good. Investigate and explore these alternatives to Craigslist. Close5 (an app or website www.Close5.com), Let Go (an app or website https://us.letgo.com/en), NextDoor (an app or website https://nextdoor.com/), Trash Nothing (an app or website https://trashnothing.com). Check out their Facebook pages also.

HOW TO ADVERTISE

The success of your sale is dependent on getting people to show up. That is the old trick of advertising. There is the old-fashioned, offline method and online methods. Online methods have no cost or low costs. There are several online sites that are popping up. There is not a *one-size fits all* that applies here. One site doesn't reach all people interested in your sale.

WHERE TO ADVERTISE

How To Post, List or Advertise a Garage Sale On Craigslist

Craigslist is a popular website for viewing and posting classified listings for jobs, sales, personals and other miscellaneous subjects. It is a simple website to navigate. It is not the most beautiful looking website but it is perhaps one of the most helpful. A lot of people go to Craigslist to enhance and market whatever business they have. To post, it is recommended (and sometimes required) that you create a free account. Having an account helps you to manage your listings and even make edits easily on listed postings.

Instructions: (Posting without the email address needed)

It is wise to draft the garage sale listing in Microsoft Word (and the like) because of its spell check feature. It is best to be professional and make your listing easy to read even when you are just going to post a garage sale listing and are not actually selling things online. A listing would include a very detailed address (from street address to any specific landmark). You also need to list your closest city and the date of your sale. You may as well include every single detail or instructions that you would want people to follow. Be polite in doing this.

The listing should also include some sample items that you have for sale and detailed descriptions of them. Uploading pictures to your Craigslist post would most likely tell the shoppers that your garage sale is worth visiting. And once this garage sale listing is compliant and ready, all you have to do is:

1. Go to www.Craigslist.com.

2. Under the heading of "United States," find your state and click on the link. Then choose the next CLOSEST city or county. Just choose the city closest in proximity.

3. On the next page, click on the link that says "post to classifieds." This link appears in the upper left-hand corner.

4. Click the "for sale," link.

5. Scroll down. Click the link that is labeled "garage & moving sales" and choose the area nearest you.

6. Enter your posting title. (Make sure that you have a catchy title that will stand out from the other postings as you're not the only one posting on the website). This also includes your city and state, the date of your sale, and the phrases "yard sale," "garage sale," or "moving sale."

7. Copy and paste your yard sale listing from Microsoft Word or Works into the "posting description" box.

8. If you took pictures of items for sales or your yard sale pile and uploaded them to your computer, go to "add/edit images."

9. Click "continue" to preview and post your yard sale listing on Craigslist.com. Your listing will appear on the website for up to 30 days. Return and remove your listing before then.

Instructions: (Posting with a use of an active email address)

1. Go to www.Craigslist.com.

2. Click the "Sign up for an Account" link at the bottom of the log in page.

3. If you don't have a Craigslist account, click the "Sign up for an Account" link at the bottom of the log in page. You'll be prompted to enter an email address and a verification code.

4. Click "create account."

5. Craigslist will send you an email with the confirmation code/link that you will need to verify your account.

6. By clicking the link sent to your email, you will then be asked to provide your password for your Craigslist account and to re-type that password. You now have a Craigslist account.

7. Click "Post to Classifieds." Select the type of posting, such as sale or job listing. Select the category for the posting. Select the general area you want to post the ad. Select a more specific location.

8. Enter a title for the posting. Enter the body text for the ad in the "Posting Description" box. Click "Hide" if you intend to put a phone number for contact in the ad or click "Anonymize" to receive email responses. To add an image, click the "Add/Edit Images" button.

9. Click "Continue." View the ad as it will be displayed to others. When it looks OK, click "Continue" or click "Edit Again" to edit the ad some more. Enter the verification code and click "Continue" to post the ad.

Pointers: Make sure to read the Terms and Agreement on the website and to post on a correct category, otherwise your post can be flagged immediately. Craigslist posts your email address anonymously.

How To Post, List or Advertise a Garage Sale On Facebook

Now that Social Networking has become commonplace, it has become very helpful in establishing and developing businesses. Facebook is perhaps one of the most famous and leading social networking site that most people have access to within their day to day activity. Placing ads on this website is also one of the best opportunities for targeted advertising. Because Facebook users provide information about their age, gender, location and interests, it is easy to target ads, such as an upcoming garage sale, directly to the demographic you want to reach.

Here is how to do it:

1. Go to www.Facebook.com/business/ads or you can also do this by visiting the Facebook website itself and simply click on the "Advertising" link at the bottom of the page.

2.   In the upper right corner Click on "Create an Ad."

3.   Insert your website or the URL where your users will be directed once they click on it.

4.   Target your advertisement/choose the demographic where you want your ad to be displayed. Select the gender, age group, educational status and other information that people in Facebook are using in order for you to categorize your target group to make it more inclusive.

5.   In the keyword section, use relevant keywords.

6.   You are now ready to create your advertisement. This is best done ahead of time. So draft it first in Microsoft Word for spelling and grammar check so that your advertisement will sound more formal.

7.   Create a short catchy title.

8.   Create a short (less than 50 words) description that will explain your product, services and advertisements.

9.   You may also add some photos by clicking the "Upload Photo."

10. You will then have the option to either have it "pay per click" or "pay per view." Click on the appropriate tab.

   •   Pay Per Click—you will only pay Facebook when someone clicks on your ad.

   •   Pay Per View—you will pay Facebook every time your ad is displayed to a user.

11. Set a budget. Indicate the amount of money you're willing to pay each day. You may pay less than this, but this is the most money you'll pay for one day of Facebook ads.

12. Bid for ad space. Facebook determines which ads to display by how much you're willing to pay per click or per 1000 impressions. Choose the maximum amount you want to pay. The amount you actually pay depends on how much other advertisers have bid, so enter the maximum amount you're willing to pay.

TIPS TO REMEMBER:

•   Click on "Test" on the left side of the Create Your Ad section to make sure your website loads properly. Clicking on "Test" will show you what the Facebook user sees when he clicks on your ad.

•   The higher your maximum bid, the more likely your ad is to be displayed.

•   Note the suggested bid amounts on the Budget section. This is the range other advertisers are currently paying for users in the demographics you chose.

•   See how many people are in your demographics by watching the number at the top of the screen in the Audience section. The number displayed is the total number of users with profiles that match the demographics you chose.

- Be sure to track your earnings and how many times people are clicking on your ads. Facebook does not monitor what users do after they click on your ad, so you need to make it your job to see if customers are buying your products or just browsing and then leaving your site.

- Make sure your ads stand out and pop. They should be bright and colorful and engage the potential customer. You don't want to bore them. Make them want more. Go beyond the typical charts and a lot of words and be crafty with your ad copy.

- Don't spam or send out mass emails. This may get your advertisement banned or do just the opposite of what you are trying to accomplish in getting potential clients.

How To Make Posts, Listings or Advertisements Using Twitterfeeds.

What is Twitterfeed?
Twitterfeed allows you to share your blog posts, advertisements, or any other content that supports RSS feeds to a wider audience via Twitter, Facebook, and LinkedIn. This means that whenever you post anything on your blog, website, or page, Twitterfeed will broadcast it on your chosen social platform sites so your friends and followers can be updated automatically about your new post without having to tweet it or post it manually.

How does Twitterfeed work?
By inputting your blog, website, or page's RSS feeds, Twitterfeed sends new items you post to your chosen social platforms (Twitter, Facebook, and LinkedIn). The format of the posts can be customized in the "Advance Settings" of your feeds.

What you need?

1. Desktop/laptop.

2. Internet connection.

3. Blogs or websites that you want to feed to your buyers.

4. Your social media platform (Facebook, Twitter, LinkedIn) that will receive the feed.

5. Know how to get the RSS feeds in case Blog URL won't parse.

Getting Started

1. Go to the Twitterfeed website http://twitterfeed.com/

2. If you already have an account, sign in with your email address and your password. Otherwise, you may create your new account by clicking in the "Don't have an account yet" link.

3. Fill in the Sign-up form by:

   a. entering your email address

   b. entering your password

   c. verifying your password

   d. you may choose to receive information and updates from Twitterfeed, or not, by checking or unchecking the provided box

   e. enter the verification code

   After signing up, you may now start creating your feed.

4. Type in the name of the blog website or the page that you want to feed on the box provided.

Enter the Blog URL or the RSS Feed URL.

In some instances, a simple URL may not parse. When this happens, you will need to enter the RSS Feed URL.

Step 1: Create Feed	Step 2: Configure Publishing Services	Step 3: Done

Thanks for signing up!

Step 1: Name Feed & Add Source URL

Feed Name

Blog URL or RSS Feed URL (help)

🔊   test rss feed

☑ Active

▶ Advanced Settings

RSS stands for Really Simple Syndication. This is what makes it possible for content publishers to syndicate a particular material across the Web (from one site to many). You may find a blog's RSS feed URL by clicking on the icon that looks like this. (Note:

▶ Advanced Settings

🕐 Update Frequency
Check for new posts [Every 30 mins ▼] And post up to [1 ▼] new update(s) at a time.

Tₜ Post Content   ☑ Post Link
Include [title & description ▼]   Shorten link through [bit.ly ▼] ▶ bitly settings

NEW: Use your own short domain for free at bitly.com!

Facebook options:
If "title & description" is selected above, we post a wall post with an automatic thumbnail. If "title only" or "description only" is selected, we post a status update with no images. If you want to post a full wall post, but without the automatic thumbnail, you can un-check the checkbox below.
☑ Include automatic thumbnails in Facebook wall posts

🔠 Post Sorting
Post new items based on [pubDate ▼]

It's usually found on top of blogs.

If this still fails, and a blog does not contain the image of RSS feed URL, you may want to check on buttons with labels of either "Atom" or "Syndicate."

If all else fails, you may want to check out the documentation of the blogging software you are using. This should tell how to get to your RSS feed URL.

5. Click on Advance Settings. This enables you to customize the posting of the feeds (i.e.

Post Prefix
Prefix each tweet with: (max. 20 characters)

Post Suffix
Suffix each tweet with: (max. 20 characters)

Keyword Filter
Separate multiple words with a space:

- To only post items that include certain words: add them below separated by a space posts that contain the word apple OR the word pear.
- To exclude posts with a certain word: prefix it wth --, eg. --apple will exclude all posts

☐ Filter your posts by using keywords to auto-approve new posts

the frequency of updates, what to include in the post, how many updates you want to feed at a time).

6. Still on Advance Settings, one of the things that you can customize is how the post will appear in your feed (via Twitter, Facebook, or both). For Twitter, you can choose to put a prefix or a suffix to each feed that Twitterfeed will post, so that each time a new update comes and feeds it on Twitter, it will have that uniform beginning or ending to each post.

For Facebook, you can choose to have each posting include a thumbnail or not, and

Facebook options:
If "title & description" is selected above. we post a wall post with an automatic thumbnail. If "title only" o selected. we post a status update with no images. If you want to post a full wall post. but without the au can un-check the checkbox below.
☑ Include automatic thumbnails in Facebook wall posts

choose whether you want it to post the title alone, or the title and description together (which is also an option for Twitter).

Since Twitter only allows posting of up to 140 characters, choosing the "title only" option is recommended since there will not be enough space for a description to be included.

Feed Publishing
http://www.simonwchan.com/feed/

Step 1: Create Feed	Step 2: Configure Publishing Services	Step 3: Done

Feed was successfully created.

Available Services

Twitter

Facebook

Linkedin

You may also choose to filter a post using keywords. When there are only certain posts from a blog that you want to feed into your chosen social platform, you can do that by entering a keyword so that only posts from a blog that contains those words (in the title and description, depending on your choice of post) will be syndicated to your social platform of choice. If you don't have limitations or constraints as to what updates will be posted, you need not mind this part:

Click on Continue to Step 2

You may now choose which social platform you want to feed posts into.

After clicking on your chosen social platform, it will ask you for authentication. If you are not yet logged in, you will need to log in using your username and password (on

Keyword Filter
Separate multiple words with a space:

- To only post items that include certain words: add them below separated by a space. eg. "apple pear" will only publis posts that contain the word apple OR the word pear.

- To exclude posts with a certain word: prefix it wth --. eg. --apple will exclude all posts with the word apple in them.

  Filter your posts by using keywords to auto-approve new posts.

Twitter) or your email address and password (on Facebook). If you are already logged in, just click on "Allow" access and then hit "Create Service."

Choose existing Twitter Account or Authenticate a new account

1. Authenticated Twitter Account
   --Twitter Account--

2. Authenticate new Twitter Account

Authenticate Twitter
Using OAuth

Authenticate with Username & Password

UTM Tags
Source: twitterfeed
Medium: twitter
Campaign:
Optional Tags
Term:

7. Click on the "All Done!" button.

8. After successfully performing the steps, you have now configured a feed. This indicates that every time there is an update from the blog you chose, there will be an automated feed that will be posted on your chosen social media platform.

Step 1: Create Feed   Step 2: Configure Publishing Services   **Step 3:** Done

Service created successfully.

Active Services

Facebook   ☑ Active

Available Services

Twitter

Facebook

Linkedin

All Done!   Back to Step 1

How To Make Posts, Listings or Advertisements Using USFreeAds www.USFreeAds.com

Placing a classified on USFreeAds couldn't be easier!

Login to your existing account or register for a new account.

Select the category you'd like your ad to be shown in.

Select the type of ad you'd like to create (HTML or text)

Type your ad content

Preview your ad and make any changes

All done—your ad is live!

Note: on this website, there is a membership option that allows you to post as many as 12 photos per add and enjoy other advertising feature add-ons with a given fee (using PayPal) however, their free advertising is good.

How To Post, List or Advertise a Garage Sale On Yardsalesearch

Yardsalesearch is a search engine that provides free posting and advertising on yard sales throughout the United States. It is where you will find garage sales, yard sales, and estate sales on a map.

Posting/ listing or advertising a Garage Sale on www.yardsalesearch.com is very, very easy. Here are the short and easy steps.

1.   Go to the website. (www.yardsalesearch.com)

2.   Click on "Post a Yard Sale."

3.   Enter a complete and correct address.

4.   Click "Check Address."

5.   Put a catchy and interesting title on your post along with the description. Make sure you include all the necessary details about the garage sale.

6.   Provide the "Start Date" and "End Date" of your garage sale.

7.   Indicate the specific time of your opening.

8.   Put in your name and email address.

9.   Also provide a password, in case you need to edit your posts.

10. Enter the verification code.

11. Lastly, click "Post My Yard Sale." And you're done!

OTHER PLACES YOU CAN PLACE CLASSIFIED ADS

Newspaper (your local newspapers' classified ad section).

PennySaver 866-640-3900 www.PennySaverUSA.com (both offline and online)

Hoobly Classifieds www.hoobly.com

eBay Classifieds www.eBayclassifieds.com

Backpage www.BackPage.com

FreeCycle www.FreeCycle.org

Garage Sales Tracker 561-372-2442 www.garagesalestracker.com

Tag Sell It www.TagSellIt.com

ONLINE AUCTIONS

There are several big online auction websites that are generalists and will sell everything. My "go to" auction website is eBay.

This site compares the online auctions: www.auctionalfie.com

This is a general auction site: www.Bonanza.com

This is a general auction site: www.IOffer.com

This is a general auction site: www.sell.com

This is a good general online auction site: www.webstore.com

This is an auction site for antiques: www.goantiques.com

This is an auction site for beads: www.justbeads.com

This is an auction site for lab equipment, and medical equipment: www.labx.com

A wine auction site: www.Winebid.com

The International Antique Shop www.TIAS.com

Selling
INDIVIDUAL ITEMS

Chapter 4
Selling Individual Items

It started out innocently enough. Then one day you turned around and there were all these eyes looking at you! Clowns' eyes, snowmen's eyes, pig's eyes . . . Mother's Day presents, Christmas presents, and whenever someone comes over they bring the dang things. What do you do now?

This chapter takes a look at the individual collections that you may have and helps you find a new home for them. It is in alphabetical order to make it easier for you to find the item. Why this list? Because these are the items I see most often when I'm working with clients.

Often when you have more than one of an item, it could be considered a collection; for instance:

1930s ceramics	Collectibles	Gentlemen's accessories
1940s fashions	Comics	Glassware
1950s fashions	Commemorative antiques	Glaze
1960s fashions	Computer games	Golf
African art and antiques	Continental furniture	Half dolls
Amberina glass	Cookie jars	Halloween collectibles
American arts and crafts	Corgi toys	Hats
American furniture	Corkscrews	Historical memorabilia
American Indian art	Costume jewelry	Hot Wheels
Animation	Cottage ware	Jadeite
Architectural antiques	Cult TV	James Bond
Autographs	Cups and saucers	Japanese ceramics
Automobilia	Decanters and cocktail	Jelly molds
Barbie	shakers	Jewelry
Barometers	Delft	Lady head vases
Baseball	Depression glass	Lamps
Beatles	Digital watches	Lead soldiers
Belleek	Dinky toys	Lusterware
Bisque dolls	Dollhouses	Marbles
Blenko	Dolls	Masks – ceramic wall
Blue Willow	Earthenware	Meissen
Blue-and-white ware	Elvis Presley	Memorabilia
Bone china	Eskimo art	Metal automobile toys
Cameras	Faberge eggs	Militaria
Carnival glass	Fabric dolls	Model trains
Ceramics	Fans	Models
Character collectibles	Fenton	Modern first editions
Children's books	Fiesta ware	Money
Chinese ceramics	Floral ceramics	Movie memorabilia
Christmas memorabilia	Football	Murano glass
Clocks	Fountain pens	Native American art
Coalport	French Limoges	New York World's fair
Coca-Cola	Furniture	Nursery playthings
Coins and paper money	Games	Nursery ware

Ocean liner memorabilia
Old brass and cooper
Kitchenalia
Oriental
Oriental antiques
Oriental ceramics
Sporting
Hello Kitty
Memorabilia
Paperback books
Paperweights
Pedal cars
Pens
Perfume bottles
PEZ dispensers
Plastic and Bakelite
Plastic dolls
Plates
Political memorabilia
Pop commemoratives
Porcelain
Post-1960s fashion
Pottery
Powder compacts
Printed ephemera (paper)
Purses
Queen Anne
Quilts

Radios and TVs
Rock and pop music
Royal Crown Derby
Royal Doulton china
Royal Doulton figurines
Royal Dux Bohemia
Royal Worcester
Royalty memorabilia
Russian antiques
Salt and pepper shakers
Scandinavian glass
Sci-Fi TV memorabilia
Scottie dogs
Sevres
Shaker
Silverware
Smoking accessories
Snow globes
Soft toys
Space memorabilia
Spode
Staffordshire china
Staffordshire figurines
Stanhopes
Star Wars
Steiff
Steuben
Stoneware and Redware

Sunglasses
Tankards
Tea sets
Teapots
Teddy bears
Telephones
The 1930s
The 1950s
The 1960s
Tiffany glass
Tinplate toys
Tins
Toby Jugs
Toys
Victorian furniture
Vintage advertising
Vintage fashions
Vintage kitchen
   equipment
Vintage magazines
Vintage packaging
Vintage posters
Vintage sewing tools
Vintage shoes
Vintage wood objects
Watches
Weather vanes

This chapter starts out with a description of the product. Then, places (brick and mortar locations) where you could sell this item. Some communities won't have this storefront, so you may need to call the store and discuss your item on the phone.

Selling online is often the best option, and breaks the geographical barrier. Some online locations have a physical location and phone number so you can call. Others may only communicate via internet, email, text messaging, etc.

If you find that you can't sell the item and want to donate it, the first donation location is a local address. The second address is an online address where you may need to ship your item (and incur a cost).

Associations, Societies and LinkedIn Groups are your versions of Who Wants To Be A Millionaire—Phone a Friend. These contacts can often lead you to people that you need to know but didn't know who to ask. To find a LinkedIn Group for your particular item go to: www.collectors.org.

Book(s) are referenced for you to do your homework. The ISBN is listed which is like a social security number for a book. All you need to do search the number and you'll find the book. You don't need to know the title, year published, spelling, etc. I comment on what I like and don't like about the book. If you're not looking for that particular information, pass on that book.

I've also included a couple of quick tips on caring for the items.

ANTIQUES

We've already defined what age an item has to be to be considered an antique, but what items are antiques? I could say anything that went into a house or a farm, so there is a large range of categories within antiquing. This is a very large category, and many, many books have been written on the subject. Furniture is also a very large section.

Storefront:
In almost every community, there is an old downtown that will have an antique and collectables area where several stores are near each other. If you don't know where this is in your area, find the antique mall/co-op. They typically have newspapers, handouts and flyers with addresses, names and phone numbers of local resources. If you are still in doubt, ask the people behind the counter.

Online:
Junkables www.junkables.com

Antique Alley www.antiquealley.com

GoAntiques www.goantiques.com

Associations, Societies and LinkedIn Groups:
"I Antique Online" LinkedIn Group

National Association of Dealers in Antiques

NAADAA, The National Antique and Art Dealers Association of America www.naadaa.org

ADA, Antiques Dealers' Association of America www.adadealers.com

ART WORK

"I don't know art, but I know what I like" makes this section very difficult. There is so much diversity in art that it makes it difficult to generalize. When you have art work, have it appraised and go to a person who specializes in that area.

Storefront:
You may want to check around in your local neighborhood and see where there are stores or boutiques. Consider putting your items on consignment—you get paid when the item is sold by the shop-keeper, after you invoice them.

Online:
Etsy www.Etsy.com

Art Brokerage www.artbrokerage.com

Yessy Art Gallery www.yessy.com

Donate:
Collectibles With Causes 888-228-7320 www.collectibleswithcauses.org/donate-art.html

Associations, Societies and LinkedIn Groups:
International Association for Professional Art Advisors 888-682-2722 (no email or website)

American Society of Artists, Inc. 312-751-2500 www.AmericanSocietyofArtists.com

---

Book:
Warman's Antiques & Collectibles Mark F. Moran 978-1-4402-0408-1. Great pricing guide. In the **front** of the book, ask an expert. Then the items are listed alphabetically.

AUTOMOBILES

Cars are a part of American life. The *cash for clunkers* program was an amazing program where many people took their older car(s) and sold them or traded them in for cash. You may still have a car or two around that you want to sell.

Storefront:
Carmax www.Carmax.com

Gulliver USA 888-831-6127 http://gulliverusa.net/ You can sell or consign your car

Online:
CashForCarsQuick 888-862-3001 http://cashforcarsquick.com

MillsMotors Inc 800-640-3236 www.millsmotors.com

Auto Rev 888-209-5611 www.autorev.com

Craigslist www.Craigslist.com

Donate:
Donation Line LLC Vehicle Donation Center 877-227-7487 www.donationline.com Their site is great for the forms, the IRS regulation regarding vehicle, whether the vehicle runs or not, and what type of vehicles (more than just autos).

DonateCarUSA 800-269-6814 www.donatecarusa.com 50 percent of the net proceeds of your car donation go to the charity

Habitat for Humanity 877-277-4344 www.habitat.org/carsforhomes/

Associations, Societies and LinkedIn Groups:
eBay Motors Classic Cars...Buy/Sell/Trade

Books:
eBay Motors The Smart Way Joseph T. Sinclair 0-8144-7252-4. Part III Personal Selling has a good resource section that gives step-by-step instructions on how to sell your vehicle on eBay.

For sale the official Auto-By-Owner used car sellers guide and handbook, a consumer publication (no author) 0961447109 [sub-title: How to Make More Money Selling Your Own Used Car] copyright 1984. Although this is an old book, it has forms for you to copy, how to price the car, how to find a wholesaler, how to find auto traders and how to detail and clean up your car for sale. I don't think I would suggest you purchase the book. If your library has it, it's worth checking out.

AVON

I thought that this was a *must have* to include. I remember my mother buying Avon products growing up. When I researched Avon, I couldn't find anything on Avon but bottles. Now that I'm writing this book, it's dawning on me that all the products were in bottles! Oh, yeah. A collection of bottles.

Storefront:
Avon Collectibles www.findavon.com

Associations, Societies and LinkedIn Groups:
National Association of Avon Collectors national association, with local chapters

BABY AND CHILDREN'S CLOTHES

Baby clothes are one of those things that do well selling. For the Children's category, a child is anyone younger than a teenager.

Baby

Storefront:
Gingersnaps Kids www.gingersnapskids.com

Once Upon A Child 614-791-1000 (clothes/toys) www.OnceUponAChild.com

Online:
Craigslist www.Craigslist.com

Stork Brokers 888-302-9243 www.storkbrokers.com

Gently-Used.com http://gently-used.com

Donate:
Donation Town www.donationtown.org multiple locations nationwide

Baby2Baby 323-933-2229 www.baby2baby.org

Donate Online:
Loved Twice 510-652-2229 http://lovedtwice.org (Recycled Clothing for Newborns in Need) only to one year old

Wellspring Family Services 206-902-4233 https://www.wellspringfs.org/get-involved/donate-clothing-other-essentials Seattle area

Children

Storefront:
Children's Orchard www.ChildrensOrchard.com

Online:
Once Upon A Child www.OnceUponAChild.com

Donate:
H&M Clothing stores www.hm.com/us

Donate Online:
Blossom Birth http://BlossomBirthCenter.com

BARBIE

Barbie was first introduced in 1959 and continues to be produced. Although the doll is highly collectible, because of the number of variations in the doll itself plus all the costumes and accessories, there are literally millions of Barbie doll variations available and the value is based on a combination of the scarcity and more importantly, the quality of the piece and whether or not it has original packaging.

Storefront:
Annette Givens, appraiser AnnetteMG@aol.com

Donate:
Article: www.ehow.com/how_6747541_donate-barbies.html

The Barbie Girls Project www.facebook.com/pages/The-Barbie-Girls-Project/135528563210747

Associations, Societies and LinkedIn Groups:
The Barbie Girls Project www.facebook.com/pages/The-Barbie-Girls-Project/135528563210747

Barbie Collector 800-491-7514 www.barbiecollector.com

Barbie Doll Collectors Club International 914-362-4657

Barbie Club Online
Modern Barbie and Fashion Doll Clubs This is a list of clubs
http://collectdolls.about.com/od/mbdollclubs/Modelrn_Barbie_and_Fashion_Doll_Clubs.htm

Barbie Fan Club (Official Mattel Site) www.barbiecollector.com

---

Books:
The Barbie Doll Years A Comprehensive Listing & Value Guide of Dolls and Accessories Patrick C. Olds 1-57432-271-0. This is an excellent book, and it just has prices.

The Barbie Closet Price Guide for Barbie & Friends Fashions and Accessories: 1959-1970 Patricia Long 0-87341-695-3. This is an excellent for prices for those years.

BASEBALL CARDS

Almost every boy and many men collected baseball cards. My brother has a collection of baseball cards still in his closet. They were going to put his daughter through college. Perhaps I should call him and see if I could get him to sell them now!

Pawn Stars is fun to watch when they have a baseball card to buy. They have to grade it and then agree on a price.

With eBay, the price and scarcity of baseball cards changes. The prices are soft right now. What helps the card's value is the have the baseball card professionally graded. This service cost is approximately $15 to $20 per card and can increase the value 40 percent per card.

Attend baseball card shows. To begin, just walk the show and learn. Pick up flyers, business cards, magazines, etc. Ask questions. Find out who's who in the industry, in your area of the country. Who is respected and trusted; who you should stay away from, what should/could you expect to get for your cards. You may only be able to sell your card at about 10 percent of the price listed in the price guide (ouch!).

The top grading companies in this field are:
Professional Sports Authenticator (PSA) www.psacard.com

Beckett Grading Service (BGS) www.Beckett.com

GMA Grading www.GMAgrading.com

Sportscard www.sgccard.com

International Grading Service (IGS) www.IGSGrading.com

Storefront:
Your local baseball card shop

A to Z cards and Collectibles 559-440-1926

Online:
Kruk Cards 248-656-8803 www.krukcards.com

SportsCardFun.com www.sportscardfun.com/we_buy_baseball_cards.asp has a list of online buyers

Donate:
Collectibles With Causes www.collectibleswithcauses.org

Cards2Kids 312-362-2452 www.cards2kids.org

Baseball Almanac www.baseball-almanac.com/support.shtml

Associations, Societies and LinkedIn Groups:
Baseball Autograph Update Group
http://groups.yahoo.com/group/BaseballAutographUpdate/

Books:
Collector Guide to Baseball Card Troy Kirk 0-87069-533-9. The main factor affecting card value profiting from baseball card has reference books in back.

The Official Beckett Price Guide to Baseball Cards 2010, Edition #30 (Beckett Official Price Guide to Baseball Card Dr. James Beckett 978-0-375-72336-0. The price guide is excellent.

BEDS AND MATTRESSES

Many homes have a bed frame lying around the house, or in the garage after a child grew up or moved out of the house.

Just for my enjoyment, I checked out what to do with your mattress. I thought that it was illegal to sell a mattress because it was used, but my research discovered that that was incorrect.

www.ehow.com/how_2124948_sell-used-mattress.html this will tell you how.

Storefront:
1-800-Used Mattress

Online:
Craigslist www.Craigslist.com

Donate:
Donation Town www.donationtown.org

You need to tell when it was used around a smoker or pets as people in fragile health can be extremely sensitive to cigarette smoke or pet hair.

Coit Carpet Cleaning company cleans mattress with a dry process if you want to clean a mattress.

Spring Back Recycling http://springbackrecycling.com/

BICYCLES

With the children grown up and a bike standing (or leaning) in the garage, it may be time to sell your two wheeler. Ah, the memories.

The difficulty in providing resources for this section is, "what's in your garage?" I am assuming that you are going to have more modern day bikes than antiques or collectible bikes.

Storefront:
Your local neighborhood shop

Wheel World Family Bikes 310-391-5251

Online:
Local Bicycle Trader 888-597-8555 www.localbiketrader.com CA

Global Bikes 480-892-1315 www.globalbikesbikeshop.com/BUYbikes.html bring it in AZ location

Once Ridden www.onceridden.com The site has selling tips and how to write a good ad

Donate:
Bikes For The World 703-740-7856 www.bikesfortheworld.org non-profit charitable

Bikeworks 206-725-9408 www.bikeworks.org/donations.php is a 501(c)3

Berkeley Parents Network http://parents.berkeley.edu/recommend/charity/bikes.html

Recycle-A-Bike 401-525-1822 www.recycleabike.org is a 501(c)3

Donate Online:
Trips For Kids 415-458-2986 www.tripsforkids.org/

BOOKS AND SCHOOL TEXT-BOOKS

It seems that every home has at least some books accumulated. They may be romance novels, sci-fi, cookbooks, business books, art, mysteries, thrillers, biography, health and fitness, nonfiction, reference, self-help, sports or travel, and boy can they stack up!

If you have a private library with a quantity of leather-bound volumes, historical titles, or art books, you may want to hire a book appraiser to value the whole collection.

Storefront:
In your area, there will be several bookstores. Call and inquire when they have a specific type of book they specialize in.

Online:
Cash4Books.net 877-243-5935 www.Cash4Books.net

Amazon www.Amazon.com

Here is how you list your book on Amazon:

On the right hand side (under the yellow "Add to Cart"), Have one to sell?

Then click "Sell on Amazon"

It will show the book that you want to sell. You don't have to do anything further here.

Describe the condition of your product.

Select the condition:
New
Used - Like New
Used - Very Good
Used - Good
Used - Acceptable

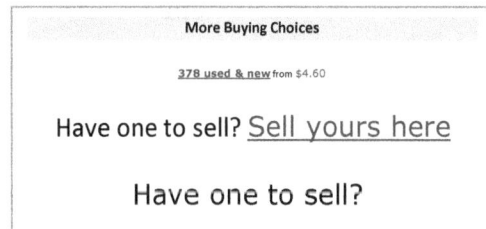

More Buying Choices

378 used & new from $4.60

Have one to sell? Sell yours here

Have one to sell?

Condition Note: Here add any little details.

Enter the price for your product. Amazon has already calculated the shipping.

Bookscouter.com http://bookscouter.com

sellbackyourBook.com 630-800-1491 www.sellbackyourbook.com

Books-FYI.com www.Books-FYI.com textbooks also

Donate:
Books for Africa www.booksforafrica.org

Donate online:
Book Aid International 44 (0) 20 7733 3577 www.bookaid.org

Associations, Societies and LinkedIn Groups:
Antiquarian Bookseller's Association of America 20 W 44th St 4th Fl New York NY 10036 212-944-8291

School Text-Books

We all went to school. Some of us even went to post-secondary school. Buying text-books at the beginning the semester often broke our bank. What do we do with the books afterwards? Use them as a boat anchor?

Storefront:
Check around the college where the text was purchased. These stores are famous for not paying high dollar for the text-books when buying back the books. They typically are only buying books that the instructors will be using the next quarter.

Donate:
Got Books? 978-416-8288 www.gotbooks.com

Caring for books: Place a layer of cheesecloth over the brush attachment of your vacuum hose, turn the power to low, and sweep front and back carefully. For smudges on book pages, use a pink eraser that you can buy at an artist's supply store.

Donate:
Local libraries may have preferences of what they wish to receive. Call the library (especially Friends of the Library) and ask what they are looking for. If they aren't interested, ask for a suggestion in your area where you could donate your books (a school, a senior community, Rotary/Kiwanis club, etc.).

Book:
Where to Sell It! Tony Hyman 0-399-51817-7. The whole book is a great reference guide. It has no internet reference.

CAMERAS

This category was a little difficult because what I often see in people's homes are old digital cameras that they want to get rid of. For that suggestion, look at similar places for computers and cell phones. An older camera would be a film camera the kind we grew up with, and will be more difficult to sell because it's too new for someone else to want to buy and use but not old enough for a collector.

In this category the age of vintage and antique will have its own time line. See previous definition of rock and hard place! An important question to ask is, "Does the camera need to be in working order?" Depending on the age, a non-working camera may be a deal breaker, or it may not matter.

You may want to attend a historical camera show for additional contacts and resources.

Storefront:
Harry Poster 201-794-9606 [Kodak and Polaroid]

Online:
Gazelle www.Gazelle.com

KEH Camera 770-333-4200 www.keh.com

Used Camera Buyer 866-735-5444 x 9 www.usedcamerabuyer.com

eBay www.eBay.com

Donate:
Recycling for Charities 866-630-7557 www.recyclingforcharities.com

Kid Camera Project www.kidcameraproject.org

Recyclers.org www.recycles.org/donate.php

Donation Town www.donationtown.org

Historic Camera http://historiccamera.com/donations.html

Donate Online:
Naylor Museum of Photographic History 617-731-6603

Associations, Societies and LinkedIn Groups:
http://cameraculture.media.mit.edu

Daguerraian Society 3045 W Liberty Ave Ste 7 Pittsburg PA 15216-2460 412-343-5525

Vintage Camera Club 2562 Victoria St Wichita KS 67216 316-265-0393

CANS/RECYCLING

In my book, *The Clutter Bug Investigates Coupons, Discounts, and Deals*, I investigated CRV (after buying sodas at great savings). It is amazing how those cans and plastic bottles can add up to dollars, and the dollars to hundreds of dollars.

Demolishing teams have known for years that there is money in them there hills.

- Trashed Recycling Store also called: scrap yard, metals recycler or demolition company.

- Paper: this includes paper, books, magazines, newspapers, catalogs, junk mail, printer paper, envelopes, gift wrapping paper, cardboard, and even paper egg cartons. Priced by the pound.

- Textiles: cotton, wool and table linen. Here is an article to help www.recyclingsuperguide.com/how-to-recycle-fabric.html.

People have washing machines, dryers, lawnmowers, grills, and many other things that have metal in them.

Online:
www.terracycle.com/en-US/ This site looks like it could work. I haven't been able to make it work for me. It is more for a school that would like to collect keyboards (for instance) as a fundraiser. There is no phone number and emails weren't returned, until I said "can I send you three keyboards and pay the shipping?" No problem, here's the address. I never heard back from them.

Donate:
Cans For Hope www.cansforhope.org Soda cans and in steel, Denver area 303-875-5700

COINS

People (numismatists) have been collecting coins for ages so some collections are valuable and some are not. Mike remembers in his youth going to the bank with $2.20. He would get four rolls of pennies and look for the ones that he needed to fill out his collection, replace those with the pennies that he brought, write his name on the wrappers, and then swap them for more pennies to review. The project was fun and the coins were worth a lot to Mike but not very much when he decided to sell them!

Like baseball cards, coins have a grade. The service for coins is The Professional Coin Grading Service (PCGS) www.pcgs.com. Coin shows are a great place for information.

To educate yourself and find contacts, find a local coin shows.

Storefront:
Heritage Auction Galleries 800-872-6467 www.ha.com

Ira & Larry Goldberg Auctioneers 800-978-2646 www.goldbergcoins.com

Stack's Bowers Galleries 800-458-4646 www.Stacksbowers.com

Online:
The Reeded Edge, Inc. 888-856-COIN www.reedededge.com

USA Coin Book www.usacoinbook.com

American Coin 800-771-2646 www.acoin.com

CoinSite Buyers www.coinsite.com/html/coinbuyers.asp

Silver Superior Coins 800-541-3462 www.silversuperiorcoins.com

Golden Eagle 800-735-1311 www.goldeneaglecoin.com

Donate:
Coinstar www.coinstar.com/donatecharity

The Coin Group 233 244 22 52 39 http://www.coingroup.org/donate-your-coins/ Ghana

Collectibles With Causes www.collectibleswithcauses.org

Donate Online:
Bust Half Dollar www.BustHalfPrices.com/bhnc.php

The Numismatic Bibliomania Society www.CoinBooks.org

Associations, Societies and LinkedIn Groups:
CoinTalk www.CoinTalk.com

American Numismatic Association www.money.org

Books:
A Guide Book of United States Coins R.S. Yeoman 978-079483347-3 This book is best for the valuation of coins.

Coin Collecting for Dummies Neil Berman 978-0-470-22275-1. Chapter 21 The Art of the Sale: Selling Your Coins Yourself (enough said).

The Official Blackbook Price Guide to US Coins 2011 49th Edition Thomas E. Hudgeons Jr. 978-0375723223.

Coin Collecting for Dummies Neil Berman 978-0-740-22275-1. This book has two chapters for Selling Your Coins. Just what we are looking for.

COKE® COCA-COLA

"I'd like to buy the world a Coke" may have been used in 1971 and buying Coke merchandise is one of the favorite pastimes of people. This is a tricky area because it is so popular. When it looks old and is in good shape, it may be because it was *re-issued*. There was a time (let's say 50 years ago) that Coke took the items that were then 30 years old and copied them. People bought them again and this time, saved them.

Storefront:
The Nostalgia Store 828-669-2205

Online:
ColaCorner.com 714-516-COKE www.colacorner.com Specializing in Coca-Cola collectibles

2CollectCola.com 877-631-2653 www.2collectcola.com/sellyourcola.html

Associations, Societies and LinkedIn Groups:
Organizations for Coca-Cola Collectors www.go-star.com/antiquing/cokeorg.htm

Coca-Cola Collectors' Club International PO Box 49166 Atlanta GA 30359-1166

Soda Spectrum www.sodaspectrum.com

Book:
Petretti's Coca-Cola Collectible Price Guide Allan Petretti 978-0896896918. The information in the back lists other books on the subject. It has a chapter on Reproductions, Newspaper and Magazines Advertising, Coolers, Clocks, Tin Signs, Calendars, Pictures/Photos. It is well worth checking out. The ISBN is for the 8th Edition, and the 11th (2001) Edition was available on Amazon. The 8th is still very informative.

CHINA

You get engaged, register your china pattern, and the only time you use your good china is during the holidays. Then the divorce occurs and the china stays packed away. Now what?

There are many patterns of china and types of dishes from every-day ware, stoneware, china and more.

Storefront:
Chinasearch 855-668-668 www.ChinaSearch.co.uk

Online:
Replacements Ltd. www.Replacements.com china, silver, and silver
selltous@replacements.com to inquire about selling your china, crystal, flatware,
hollowware, or collectibles.

Donate Online:
American Institute for Conservation

China, Glass and Giftware Association

Associations, Societies and LinkedIn Groups:
Carr China Collectors' Club www.carrchina.com

Caring for china: To remove tea and coffee stains rub with a mixture of salt and vinegar.
Browning occurring from age can be removed from household bleach.

CLOTHES

We all have old clothes, clothes we never wear, clothes that don't fit, clothes of a different
fashion style, and clothes that were a gift, just sitting in the closet taking up space. Why not
make some room and sell some clothes?

Storefront:
Plato's Closet www.PlatosCloset.com

Buffalo Exchange http://buffaloexchange.com/

Online:
Hoobly Classifieds www.hoobly.com

Overstock www.Overstock.com
The information that they look for on each item is: brand, product name, product
description, MSRP, regular wholesale price, offering price, quantity offered, FOB point,
current retailers selling this product, and price sold at other retailers.

Donate:
Out of the Closet http://outofthecloset.org/

Book:
How to Sell Clothing, Shoes, and Accessories on eBay Charlene Davis 1-599180-05-7. This is
a good book especially when you're going to be selling a lot of clothes on eBay. It's for a
business, and it has a how to list and this is so helpful!

Vintage Clothes (1980)

Storefront:
Vintage Tends www.vintagetrends.com

Buffalo Exchange http://buffaloexchange.com/

Online:
Ballyhoo Vintage Clothing 877-295-6838 www.ballyhoovintage.com

Rusty Zipper 866-387-5944 www.rustyzipper.com

Vintage Vixen 941-627-2254 www.vintagevixen.com

ModCloth www.modcloth.com

Vintage Clothing Store Canoga Park www.poshgirlvintage.com

Donate:
Country Living www.countryliving.com/antiques

Bank & Vogue 613-747-8465 x 178 www.bankvogue.com/vintage-clothing/

Out of the Closet http://outofthecloset.org/

Donate Online:
American Kidney Services, Inc. 770-872-4260 www.akspickup.org/donate_vintage.html

Associations, Societies and LinkedIn Groups:
Vintage Fashion & Costume Jewelry Club www.lizjewel.com

Books:
The Little Guide to Vintage Shopping Melody Fortier 978-1-59474-404-4 This book has a great resource by state! It also talks about storing and caring for antique garments.

Born-Again Vintage Bridgett Artise 97-0-307-40527-2. A reference section with Vintage Stores in back. The reference section is interesting and may be helpful. It has auctions and expositions (not exactly what we're looking for [selling], organizations, mail-order dealers [who you may be able to sell to] periodicals, and organizations. When you have hit a dead end, THEN, this may be useful.

After A Fashion Frances Grimble 0-9636517-0-6. It has a chapter on how to repair clothes (only good if you are handy with a needle and thread). A good reference section.

COMPUTERS

Often times with computers, we are upgrading them every couple of years. And what do we do with the old one? Hand-me-downs to other members of the family, schools or the community are often a solution; here are other suggestions.

Online:
Gazelle www.Gazelle.com (Apple computers)

eBay www.eBay.com

Donate:
Computers With Causes 888-228-7320 www.computerswithcauses.org

InterConnection.org 866-621-1068 www.interconnection.org

Global Crisis Solution Center www.globalcrisis.info/computerrecycle.html

Recycle Computers 4 Cancer 781-789-5413 www.recyclecomputers4cancer.org is a 501(c)3

Donate Online:
American Kidney Services, Inc. 770-872-4260 www.akspickup.org/donate_vintage.html

DISNEYANA

Many of us have loving memories of Disneyland, Disney World, have watched a Disney movie and have fond memories of all things Disney. Mike's first trip to Disneyland was in 1956, just a few months after Disneyland opened; he remembers buying Disney *stuff* even then. Since Disney pioneered the concept of licensing with the Mickey Mouse watch in the 1930s and all of the Davy Crockett® products in the 1950s, Disney memorabilia has been around for a long time. It's highly recognizable and since there's a lot of it out there, it may just be collectible and not very valuable. Disneyana is considered pop culture.

Storefront:
Sign of the Tymes Mill Antiques Center 12 Morris Farm Rd Lafayette NJ 07848 973-383-6028 www.millantiques.com

Online:
Imagineer's Marketplace 907-903-9406 http://imagineersmarketplace.com

Phil Sears Collectibles LLC 949-643-8376 www.phil-sears.com

The Mouse Man Ink www.mouseman.com

Bonanza www.Bonanza.com

Walt Disney Art Classic 305-238-4438 www.disneyclassics.net

Associations, Societies and LinkedIn Groups:
Walt Disney Collectors' Society 800-932-5749

Books:
Disneyana: Walt Disney Collectibles Cecil Munsey 978-0801521386. Although the copyright is 1974, there is enough **background** or base information, that this book could be a maybe for your research. Could provide a kernel of information or understanding.

Stern's Guide to Disney Collectibles Michael Stein 0-89145-369-5. For older items this is good. It has picture and prices. The copyright is 1989 and there is no reference section.

CDs AND DVDs

One of the neat things about CDs and DVDs is that they never (well almost never) wear out. Which makes them a great item to sell.

Storefront:
Best Buy Electronics www.BestBuy.com

DVD Empire www.dvdempire.com

Game Stop www.GameStop.com

Online:
Morninglory Music www.CashForCDs.com They pay 1st Class Postage. Require the front and back cover of CD, DVD or game.

Secondspin www.secondspin.com

Game Stop www.GameStop.com

Gazelle www.Gazelle.com

Glyde http://glyde.com (games, DVD, CDs, book)

Donate:
GreenDisk 800-305-3475 www.greendisk.com

DVDs To The Troops www.dvdstothetroops.org

FORMAL WEAR

What's lurking in the dark corners of your closet? Dresses from your long ago, from parties past, from distant affairs, always a bride's maid, and other nightmares. With women's formal wear, the irony is that the better you look in the dress, the less often you could wear it. Men have the same tuxedos; they can be worn for years. Princess Diana was the first royal to re-wear her clothes. Diana never wore the exact same outfit twice. The accessories would change. And even she eventually sold her clothes at auction! Only after Prince William suggested it.

Online:
PreOwned Wedding Dresses www.preownedweddingdresses.com

Donate:
Cinderella Dreams   Glass Slipper Project
Cinderella Project (The)   Gowns for Girls
Cinderella's Closet   Inside the Dream
Cinderella's Trunk   My Fairy Godmother
Dress for Success   Operation Fairy Dust
Enchanted Closet (The)   Priceless Gown Project
Fairy Godmother Project   Princess Project (The)
Fairy Godmothers   Ruby Room (The)
Fairy Godmothers Inc

FURNITURE

After my parents died, Mike and I inherited a couple pieces of furniture. Although I don't plan to sell them and would like them to stay within the Miller clan. I have had them appraised and restored/repaired.

One piece, which is now an antique, is my father's wooden high chair. What was fun for me was when I went back through my mother's and my photograph albums and found pictures of my brother in the high chair, myself in the high chair, and my niece in the high chair. Now I told the story of the chair, so that when it is passed down, the next generation will know its story.

The other piece of furniture is a nice table. I believe that my dad may have picked it up at the dump or at an auction. It has not been in the family *for generations*. I do love solid wood furniture. It's beautiful. My mother had a mother-in-law tongue plant in an antique water pitcher and bowl and the wood had water damage. So we had the table refinished. The guy said that the piece was nice and unique. I love the claw feet of the table.

Like art-work, the variations and styles of furniture are numerous. I would suggest taking pictures of your furniture and finding local sources. What type of furniture do you have and where would the best place to sell it? Used furniture could be sold as an antique or at a second-hand store.

Storefront:
Antique stores, consignment stores, garage sales, and used furniture dealers

In your community, there will be an antique district. Visit the vendors and ask around.

Online:
Craigslist www.Craigslist.com

eBay www.eBay.com

Donate:
Article: www.moneycrashers.com/where-donate-furniture-charity/

Donation Town www.donationtown.org/news/donate-furniture.html

Habitat for Humanity www.habitat.org/restores

Furniture Bank Association of North America www.furniturebanks.org

Associations, Societies and LinkedIn Groups:
American Institute for Conservation of Historic & Artistic Works http://aic.stanford.edu

---

Book:
How to Sell Antiques and Collectibles on eBay … and Make a Fortune! Dennis L. Prince 0-07-144569-2. This book has a good section for eBay. Has a bit of information on: grading, provenance, authentication, appraisals, care, storage, restoration, and paying for an appraisal. Has good general information for furniture, pottery, tabletop (dinnerware), stemware and flatware.

GIFT CARDS

Have you found yourself with a few too many gift cards in your drawers? Either ones that you purchased to give as gifts or ones that people have given you that didn't quite hit their mark? Or gift cards that still have a balance on that are still hanging around? Not planning to use them anytime soon, why not sell them?

Before you can sell the card, first verify the balance remaining on the card. The toll free number of each store is listed on the website. We tried to sell a gift card that only had $5 and none of them were interested. $10 was often the lowest and often $20 was want they wanted or more.

This category was fun for me to research and was a crossover both for the Clutterology® and The Clutter Bug Investigates Coupons, Discounts and Deals. Why don't you BUY discounted gift cards for your Christmas or birthday list? Do you shop at CVS/pharmacy, and then buy a gift card to use for yourself and start saving money!

Cardpool www.CardPool.com Sell gift cards for up to 92 percent cash back and get free shipping on all transactions.

Card Cash www.CardCash.com Buys outright for a discounted face value.

Swapagift www.swapagift.com They have storefronts (check cashing) where you can take the gift card for cash.

Coupon Trade 888-838-5847 www.CouponTrade.com There is a 10 percent commission.

Donate:
Gift Card Donor www.GiftCardDonor.com 75 percent of the revenues from the donated card goes to the charity.

GOLD

If you have ever gone through an airport securing screening, and you were wearing your gold jewelry and set off the machine, you found out you weren't wearing gold. With current gold prices high right now, many people are going through their drawers and finding pieces of gold and cashing in. How about you?

Things that could be gold: bracelets, broken or bent chains, broken or single earrings, bridgework, crowns, dental caps, fillings, and gold teeth, charms and pendants, class rings, jewelry made from coins, engagement rings, foreign gold coins, gold bangles, old rings, outdated items, service pins, gold watches, and wedding rings.

Storefront:
Check with your local jeweler and see if they will offer you a fair price.

Check with the offers in your local newspaper.

Online:
Monex Precious Metals 800-444-8317 www.monex.com

GROUPON

Groupon, Living Social or the daily deal websites have become the new thing. Get the deal while it's hot. The price is too good to pass up. So we grab it and there it sits and sits. But wait, your good deal is about to expire and you just don't have the time now to get around to it. You have wasted that money. Or have you? There are now websites that will buy your offer (at a discount). See also Gift Cards as there are a couple of resources there.

Online:
Coup Recoup http://couprecoup.com you can sell your daily deals.

HANDMADE CRAFTS

Part of the story that I haven't told you about my dad and his barn and our farm (where do you think barns are?), was that just on the other side of our property was a factory that made wood furniture. Every evening, Dad would dumpster dive and haul out wood, chair arms, chair legs, chair seats, etc. and bring them back to the barn. Then he would carry them up to the empty hayloft.

Over the course of years, those pieces of wood became whole chairs and he would sell them. Our hometown had a craft fair each fall, and Dad had a booth where he sold his woodworking projects. One year, Mike and I gave Dad a branding iron with his name; it said hand crafted by Leonard Miller.

Your projects may be bead work, jewelry, knitting, crocheting, or making clothes. A great thing about the internet is that it gives you a wonderful place to sell your items, or the items left at your doorstep!

Storefront:
You may want to talk with local merchants and see whether they are interested in purchasing or consigning your product.

Attend craft shows

Online:
Etsy www.Etsy.com

Donate Online:
The Dreaming Zebra Foundation 503-206-6400 www.dreamingzebra.org

Books:
How to Sell Your Crafts Online Derrick Sutton 978-0-312-54126-2. This is a good book for selling Etsy. In addition, Chapter 4 writing listings that Sell. Chapter 5 A Crash Course in Photography Both chapters will be good for any online selling that you may be doing!

Crafting As a Business Wendy W. Rosen 978-0801986321. The Yellow pages in the back are great (they're actually yellow).

JEWELRY

Have you made some jewelry that is lying around in your drawers or hanging around in your closet? Do you have a bunch of old stuff in tucked away spots? Your jewelry may be a good thing to sell.

Storefront:
Your local jewelry store, pawn shop, thrift store and craft show.

Online:
Cash4Gold.com 877-465-3590 or 800-241-1811 www.Cash4Gold.com

eBay www.eBay.com

Craigslist www.Craigslist.com

Associations, Societies and LinkedIn Groups:
The National Association of Jewelry Appraiser PO Box 655 Annapolis MD 21401 401-897-0889 www.najaappraisers.com

Jewelers of America, Inc. www.jewelers.org

Book:
100 Years of Collectible Jewelry Lillian Baker 0-89145-0661 a fair reference section

---

MUSICAL INSTRUMENTS

Many families thought that music lessons for Junior were a good idea. Junior left the house and the instrument is still around. The instrument has not yet reached vintage age, so what do you do with it?

Storefront:
Check with your local music stores.

Local public school music teachers.

Music Go Round www.musicgoround.com

Online:
Hoobly Classifieds www.hoobly.com

Donate:
The Salvation Army has an extensive musical program teaching officers and children how to play. When you want your instrument to go to a good home, contact your local Salvation Army—not necessarily the donation center.

Operation Happy Note 122 E Lincoln Ave Fergus Falls MN 56537 218-736-5541

Donate Online:
The Dreaming Zebra Foundation 503-206-6400 www.dreamingzebra.org

Associations, Societies and LinkedIn Groups:
American Musical Instrument Society www.amis.org

Books:
Maloney's Antiques & Collectibles Resource Directory David J. Maloney, Jr. 0-87349-732-5 This directory has over 20,000 listings, 11,000 websites, 14,000 email addresses, and includes experts, dealers, buyers, clubs and appraisers. Just about everything you'll need.

Where to Sell It! Tony Hyman 0-399-51817-7. The whole book is a great reference guide.

Caring for Your Family Treasures Heritage Preservation James S. Long 0-8109-2909-0 Very short list for tools for cleaning, displaying and storing. Musical instruments and taking care of them. Not where to sell it. Also includes caring for: silver, furniture, wedding dresses, video tapes, and film. These sections are small.

ORIENTAL RUGS

In recent years, there seems to be Oriental rug stores in every neighborhood. Of the few things that Mike brought with him from his first marriage, there were a couple of area Oriental rugs. Since rugs and I don't mix, we didn't keep them too long. I don't remember how we got rid of them (Goodwill?).

Storefront:
Artex Rug Gallery LA 310-659-4530

Online:
The Rug Affair & Antique Rug Co. www.spongobongo.com

Donate:
Weaving Art Museum & Research Institute

Associations, Societies and LinkedIn Groups:
The Haji Baba Club www.hajjibaba.org

National Association of Area Rug Importers, Wholesalers & Manufacturers
http://rugknot.com or www.ORIA.org

American Conference on Oriental Rugs www.acor-rugs.org

Book:
Official Price Guide to Oriental Rugs Joyce C. Ware 0-676-60023-9. This book has excellent resources.

PICTURES

From the day you are born, it seems pictures are taken of you or by you. What do you do with them now? In some cases, they may bring you some money. In this category, we are looking at non-art work photos. They may be pictures of people, from war or historical events.

Donate:
Historic Camera http://historiccamera.com

POSTCARDS

I thought this category was a must. Growing up, when my folks took us on trip, I bought postcards. They were great. There were so many postcards to choose from. I figure there are thousands of other people with postcard collections.

When researching postcards, I found the rock and hard place defined my research. Most postcards are from 1900's (the old stuff), not the 1970s and 1980s, you know . . . back when.

Associations, Societies and LinkedIn Groups:
Postcard Collecting Clubs
www.oldpostcardsforsale.com/PostcardEducation/postcard_collecting_clubs.htm

---

Book:
The Encyclopedia of Antique Postcards Susan Brown Nicholson 0-87069-730-7. This is about and for antique postcards. It has a great glossary and bibliography. It does have a price guide.

RECORD (VINYL) ALBUMS

It seems like record albums are caught in the in between stage. At one point not too long ago, they were dead and buried. People were tossing them out, finding creative ways to use them as wall art, and giving them away. Now, there are individuals that like, nay, prefer records over digital.

Storefront:
Look for the places that buy and sell CD's. They may also buy record albums, or know who in the area does.

Online:
Amazon www.Amazon.com Turn to page 45 to learn how to list your book.

Associations, Societies and LinkedIn Groups:
Record Collectors Guild www.recordcollectorsguild.org

Books:
Trash or Treasure: How to Find the Best Buyers of Antiques, Collectibles and Other Undiscovered Treasures Hyman, Tony 0-837111-03-1. This book has a couple of places for records.

Hyman's Trash or Treasure Dr. Tony Hyman 0-937111-03-1. This book actually has some information on LP records.

SHOES

How many pairs of shoes does a women need? When you ask her husband, the answer will be much different than the wife's!

Often, the closet (or whatever surface the pair of shoes lands on) will have shoes that don't fit, don't look good or just don't! With the internet, it is possible to recoup some of your money.

Online:
Hoobly Classifieds www.hoobly.com

Donate Online:
Soles4Souls, Inc. 866-521-7463 www.Soles4Souls.org is a 501(c)3

SILVERPLATED FLATWARE

You get married; you get fine china and silverware. Or someone dies and you inherit it! You only bring it out on *good* occasions. It stays in the drawer.

Online:
Replacements 800-737-5223 www.Replacements.com

Associations, Societies and LinkedIn Groups:
Society of American Silversmiths www.silversmithing.com

Caring for silver: don't wash in dishwasher; don't use the dip silver cleaning solution. Wright's Silver Polish is a good brand. Dampen the piece with white vinegar, sprinkle with salt, and then gently, ever so gently rub it with a sponge thoroughly dampened with vinegar.

Books:
Silver Plated Flatware Revised 4th Edition Tere Hagan 0-89145-428-4. When you want to price each piece or to identify the pattern that you inherited, the book is great. The beauty of the book is how simple it is. It has an index of marks and is great when you're learning about marks.

Miller's World Encyclopedia of Antiques Judith and Marin Miller 0-670-82060-1 Has good sections on silver, antique toys and furniture.

SPORTS EQUIPMENT

Most garages have some sort of sports equipment: golf equipment, bowling balls, skis, scuba equipment, tennis rackets, basket balls, soccer balls and more.

Storefront:
Play It Again Sports www.playitagainsports.com

Online:
Craigslist www.Craigslist.com

Donate:
Sports Gift 949-388-2359 www.sportsgift.org

Golf Balls

This was one that I just picked up for the fun of it. You may have them around the house or it could be a project for your kids.

Knetgolf 877-563-8877 www.knetgolf.com/topic/43-we-buy-used-golf-balls.aspx $0.90 a ball

SPORTS MEMORABILIA

With as many sports-fans as Americans have, sports memorabilia is a large category. This category also includes Olympic memorabilia. The caution here is the difference between memorabilia and sport merchandising. Just a couple of years ago, prices were higher.

Storefront:
Go to your local storefront. It may be a baseball card store.

Online:
eBid http://us.ebid.net/

STUFFED ANIMALS

Many homes have stuffed animals lying around. I know that Mike and I have accumulated several very innocently. A couple of years ago, we went to Disneyland's California Adventure and played some arcade games. We were the only two playing, so one of us was bound to win. I think that day we came home with seven stuffed animals. I haven't been able to find any places to sell stuffed animals.

Many charities won't take stuffed animals anymore. Period. No further explanations. Some charities don't have any restrictions. Then, other charities have minor guidelines. So here are some typical concerns:

I have read that when they come from a smoke free and pet free home they can be donated. At one time, I took a stuffed animal to my local dry cleaner as they had some experience cleaning them. If you spray with antiseptic to get rid of the bugs, it may help, it may not.

- Condition.

    Are there stains or discolorations, pilled or damaged clothing? Do not wash the stuffed animals or attempt to repair them.

    Caring for stuffed animals: Cornstarch is the best medium for cleaning old stuffed animals whose pile is dirty. Rub it gently into the pile with your fingers, and then let it rest overnight. The next day shake the animal gently, and then carefully brush out any remaining cornstarch with a soft brush.

    Are there any smells? Smoke or pet odors are the most common. If you live in a home with smoke (fire place, pipe smoker, cigar smoker or cigarette smoker) or have animals, you may no longer be aware of these smells. Even a stuffed animal from an environment that has a lot of dust could affect someone's allergies.

- Battery compartments.

    These guys are so cute! They dance, they sing, they boogie. The charity may not accept the stuffed animal if the animal contains any battery compartment what so ever.

- Stuffed animals that make noises. Such as singing, reciting prayers, etc.

Beanie Babies were one of those items that people thought would go up in value. They are still around and oh so cute. But they're not so cute when you're trying to sell them for a pittance.

Online:
Stuffed Animals for Emergencies, Inc. 937-708-0251
www.StuffedAnimalsforEmergencies.org

Loving Hugs, Inc. 303-948-0552 www.LovingHugs.org We have donated to this organization.

Donate:
Stuffed Animals for Emergencies, Inc. 937-708-0251
www.StuffedAnimalsforEmergencies.org not a 501(c)3

Gleaning for the World, Att: Teddy Bear Brigade, 7539 Stage Rd/PO Box 645, Concord, VA 24538

TIMESHARES

There is currently a surplus of timeshares for sale as most people are not buying them at this time. Cut your costs as much as possible by listing your timeshare independently and without the use of lawyers and agencies. The internet has made selling easy even for the most business-challenged individuals.

The best tips for selling a timeshare property are to emphasize the location, demand, season, and the price.

Before you decide to sell you timeshare you need to come to terms with the fact that if it was purchased directly from the resort or builder, you will most likely lose about 75 percent of your buying price when you sell. Sometimes it's best to cut your losses.

Keeping Your Timeshare?

When you bought your timeshare, it probably felt like a great opportunity to enjoy a luxury for just a little bit of the cost. In fact, it may still feel like that.

Question #1: How badly do you need the money? When you need the money from your timeshare in order to pay for your wife's surgery, or to help fund your child's education, you definitely have a better idea of whether you should keep your timeshare. In this case, your priorities need to be clear: family comes first, money and luxury come second.

Question #2: How much use have you gotten out of your timeshare? Without a financial crisis looming for you, you may simply wonder how much you've been enjoying your timeshare. Do you use it enough to justify the investment, or do you just, well, own it? It doesn't take a genius to figure out that cutting the fat out of your financial life can improve things for you.

Question #3: Would you rather put the money someplace else?

If you decide you want someone else to sell your timeshare for you, one of the most important steps is finding an appropriate agency that specializes in selling timeshares. Some agencies may ask you for a fee upfront and then promise you results if you pay it. Don't believe it!

Selling your timeshare never require an upfront fee unless it is a minimal ($15-$30) to list your timeshare in an online website or publication.

The main thing you need to look into before deciding to list your timeshare for sale is what other similar properties have gone for in the same area in the past year or so. This will give you a better idea of what price you can realistically expect to get for your timeshare, as well as an estimate of how long you can expect the property to sit on the market.

Do I Need To Use A Realtor?

While most people prefer to have a professional's advice when trying to sell a timeshare, there are many ways to handle the sale yourself. Several websites exist that are specifically geared towards individuals wishing to rent or sell their timeshares. Some people have even been able to sell their timeshare back to the property itself. Also, never underestimate the power of word of mouth. Tell all your friends, family members, and co-workers about the property. Even if they aren't interested in it themselves, they may know someone who is.

If you are not comfortable handling the advertising, negotiating, and sale of the timeshare yourself, a realtor is, in fact, your best bet. There are many who specialize in handling timeshares and vacation properties. They are also more familiar with the ins and outs of part-time properties than traditional realtors are. Talk to your realtor. If they don't sell timeshare, ask for a referral. Don't search the internet for "timeshare realtor" as you may get to something close to a scam.

The Bottom Line

You've visited your timeshare and realize it just isn't something you could get enough future use of to justify the ongoing expense. You aren't willing to deal with the hassle that may come from renting your timeshare out just to break even every year.

You understand you may take a loss but you also know you won't have the added expense going forward. You've made your decision whether you want to list the property yourself or have a professional do it for you. If you're going to sell it yourself, get started now. If you prefer to rely on a professional realtor, start making calls now to find a specialist in your area.

Watch out for this con: the company listing the timeshare wants (needs) your vacation week of timeshare to show it, what actually happens is that they rent it out, leaving you nothing—not even the joy of the vacation at the property.

Online:
The Timeshare Users Group 904-298-3185 www.Tug2.net

Books:
Timeshare Condominiums for the Beginner Michael Strauss 0-533-11038-6. This is a book I'm going to recommend and I may recommend that you buy it (I needed to get it as an inter-library loan). It has so much information for Advice on Selling Timeshares, Listing With a Real Estate Agency, more information about TUG, talks about scams for resale, where to report scams. The information in buried within the book and there is no index.

Used Timeshares A Guide for Buying, Using, Exchanging, Renting and Disposing of Timeshare Lee W. Lacy 978-1-4269-7395-6. This is the only book I purchased for this project. Disposing of Your Timeshare is 23 pages. In those few pages, there is a lot of meat (information). In addition, it has specific information about donating your timeshare to a charity and whether it would really help the charity. Before you stop paying the fees on your timeshare, or deeding it back. It goes into details about setting a price, finding a charity, and the ever-present scams.

TIRES

There always seems to be tires piled around buildings. You can make some money from selling them. $1.00 to $1.50 for every good passenger tire casing and up to $40 or more for large truck tire casings.

Find a store/company in your area that specializes in tire retreading. They often buy the old tires.

While you're on the phone, ask each shop you talk to if it has any restrictions on the type or number of tires you bring in. Some retreaders, for instance, won't take steel belted radials, others aren't set up to handle some sizes of casings, and other recappers have a limited capacity.

I was able to find *retreading* on Switchboard (www.Switchboard.com internet phone book—find phone number and business). I called a couple of dealers. They were more interested in truck tires than car tires. The second guy laughed at me (a knowing laugh) when I asked him what I should do with the car tires in my backyard. "Clean them up, hose them down and sell them at a yard sale" was his advice.

My recommendation, although you can make money selling tires, it might be just best to recycle them.

Online:
Recycler's World www.recycle.net/assn/index2.html

Retreading in yellow pages

TOOLS

If you have a car, a house, or are male (not exclusively) you may have tools lying around the house. When you're good at with your hands, you may have two or three of each tool (or more). Tools are an item that can be sold! Tools sell great at garage sales.

Online:
Craigslist www.Craigslist.com

TOYS

What was it about our childhood that made us hang onto our toys? When we couldn't hang onto our toys, we tended to re-purchase them when we got older and had more room and money. Toys are highly collectible when in very good condition.

Storefront:
Atomic Age 318 E Virginia Rd Fullerton CA 92831 714-446-0736

Frank & Son Collectible Show 19649 San Jose Ave City of Industry CA 91748 www.frankandsonshow.net Wednesdays 3:00 pm to 9:00 pm Saturdays 9:00 am to 5:00 pm

Litwin Antiques PO Box 5865 Trenton NV 08638-0865 609-265-1427

Milezone's Toys 270-761-8697 www.milezone.com

Online:
Kid to Kid www.KidtoKid.com

Once Upon A Child www.OnceUponAChild.com

Mothers of Pre-Schoolers MOPS 303-733-5353 www.mops.org

Donate:
Donation Town www.donationtown.org/donation-pick-up.html

Television Show:
Toy Hunter, Jordan Hembrough, 2012 to present, Travel Channel, 30 minutes. This show is all about toys and Jordan is very knowledgeable. We found the show just a little slow.

Book:
Garage Sale Millionaire Aaron LaPedis 0-9755398-4-1. Talks about what is and is not of value (beanie babies, family bible, comic books after 1970, old magazines, old newspapers). Great book when you have antique firearms, action figures (how to grade them).

VIDEO GAMES

Video games have been around for many years. Kids (of all ages) grow out of video games very quickly. You will get a better price on your video the sooner you take it in. So don't wait.

Storefront:
GameStop www.GameStop.com

Secondspin www.secondspin.com

Online:
Gazelle www.Gazelle.com

Amazon www.Amazon.com Turn to page 45 to learn how to list your book.

eBay www.eBay.com

Craigslist www.Craigslist.com

Donate:
local library

Television Show:
Collection Intervention, Elyse Luray, 2012 to present, SyFy Channel, 1 hour. I enjoy this show and learn a lot from how to store a collection, downsize and select pieces that may increase in value, to selling pieces and displaying pieces.

Saying Goodbye
TO YOUR STUFF

Chapter 5
Saying Goodbye To Your Stuff

Y ou have tried everything you could, and have been unable to sell a few items. Now it is time to say goodbye to your items by donating them to a good home.

RENT YOUR STUFF

Let me take a little side step here. Before you donate the item(s), here are websites that rent item(s). I believe that in the future, there will be more websites very similar to these. Depending on your item and your location, you may be able to get a few clams by renting it out before you donate it.

Any Hire http://anyhire.com/

FREECYCLE

As the name implies, FreeCycle www.FreeCycle.org is the act of giving away items instead of trashing them.

Pros:
- Helps the environment instead of filling up the landfills.

- Gets to someone that needs or wants the item without them having to pay (if you give the item to a charity who sells the item).

- If you are near a university or college, FreeCycle tends to be more active and better.

Cons:
- Craigslist gives you an opportunity to give things away also.

- FreeCycle uses Yahoo Groups.

In recent years, there have been several apps that have popped up and are quite good. Investigate and explore these alternatives to Freecycle. Close5 (an app or website www.Close5.com), Let Go (an app or website https://us.letgo.com/en), NextDoor (an app or website https://nextdoor.com/), Trash Nothing (an app or website https://trashnothing.com). Check out their Facebook pages also.

CHARITY STORE

Charity shops usually sell mainly used goods donated by the public and are often staffed by volunteers.

RESALE STORE

A resale shop is the phrase most often used for stores that buy their merchandise outright from individual owners. A consignment or thrift shop (Not For Profit) can also be called a resale shop, but ONLY a store that actually consigns their inventory can be called a consignment store.

All shops which sell gently-used goods are resale shops. A resale shop will purchase merchandise outright for cash.

THRIFT STORE

A thrift store is a nonprofit store that accepts donations. The proceeds usually benefit a worthy cause. Check to see if they are a 501(3)c.

The Thrift Shopper www.thethriftshopper.com This is a website that has a directory of thrift stores.

CHARITABLE DONATIONS STORES

Many of us are familiar with the big, local charities that accept donations. I have included three here plus additional information about these organizations that you may or may not know.

General Donations: a place where you can donate almost anything and everything.

The Salvation Army

Pros:
- They will pick up your donation.
- They have locations near you.
- They will take large items like sofas.

Cons:
- Sometimes they are very selective about what they accept.
- They sell your stuff.
- They toss a bunch of what is donated.

Here is a donation value guide.
The Salvation Army www.satruck.org/donation-value-guide

Goodwill

Pros:
- They will pick up your donation.
- They have locations near you.
- They will take large items like sofas.
- They put people to work.

Cons:
- Sometimes they are very selective about what they accept.
- They sell your stuff.
- They toss a bunch of what is donated.

The Jewish Women's Council

Pros:
- Great itemization receipt for your records
- Staffed by volunteers

Cons:
- They have fewer locations
- May not pick up your items

Other organizations you may be familiar with and may pick-up your donations: Big Brothers and Big Sisters, Habitat for Humanity, hospice organizations, humane societies, Out of the Closet and the Vietnam Veterans organizations. In addition, in your local neighborhood, there are charity shops, thrift stores, and second-hand stores.

CHARITIES

As you are going through closets, drawers, or the garage and find good items that you would like to donate, but feel that The Salvation Army or Goodwill is not appropriate we have created a list for these special items.

This list of charities (and a couple of businesses) has been compiled with the assistance from students that have taken our seminars, which is why many of the charities are located in California. The criteria of including the charity in the listing was the charity was looking for more than your money or your time. They were looking for specific items (mostly used, some have specified new).

There are two ways to use this list. The first is by Alphabetical by Item. If you are looking to donate eyeglasses, look at the chart for the word eyeglasses. The right hand column provides the name of charities wanting eyeglasses. To find the address, telephone number, and website, go to the end of the Alphabetical by Item chart.

The second way is by cause. If you want to support Shared Bread, the contact information is listed and all the items they're in need of.

In either case, call or go to the website of the charity. Ask how they accept donations (will they pick it up or do you need to make arrangements to get it to them)? If the charity is geographically undesirable (too far to drive), ask if they have a closer/local contact? You may choose to ship the item(s) to the charity.

We have also included the non-profit 501(c)3 status. We weren't able to find the 501(c)3 for every listing. The charity may be operating under their primary charity (Books For Soldiers is operated by Red Grail Ministries). Religious organizations don't have 501(c)3. A couple of charities operate with several charities and you will get a donator letter after you make your donation. The listing may be a referral service to a charity. There are even a couple of international charities and businesses. You can do further research at http://501c3lookup.org/.

In looking over the list, you may come up with charities that you know (but had momentarily forgotten) about. Or you may come up with your own creative idea. For instance, schools are always in need of items as simple as pens and pencils. Contact a school or a department for donating items. Drama and theater departments may need clothes and items to use as props on stage.

If you'd like your donations to support a local women's shelter however the location of the shelter is not available. Talk to the police department, fire department, or ministers, as they may be able to coordinate your donations. Many police stations provide drop-off for donations.

For a more up-to-date list, visit www.Clutterology.com Donations [Finding New Homes for Your Good Items]

Although all the items are items you have previously purchased, when the words "to recycle" are used, that means that the item is obsolete and will be stripped down, disassembled and dismantles for parts and components.

Item	Charity
airline miles	NW/Delta 800-327-2881, World Craniofacial Foundation
aluminum foil	Safe Nest Shelter
appliances	Healing Tree Arts, Harbor Interfaith Shelter, Patriots and Paws
appliances to recycle	ASBA
art and crafts supplies such as canvases, gray sculpting clay, paint acrylic (water based, ½ gallon bottles or larger), paint glitter, paint tempra	Camp To Belong, Free Arts for Abused Children, Mend
art work	Collectibles With Causes
baby: bottles and bottle brushes, blankets, clothes, diaper cream, diapers, food, formula, items, lotion, Pedialyte, powdered Similac formula, shampoo, sippy cups, soap, wipes, pacifiers	Baby2Baby, Blossom Birth, Donation Town, Free Arts for Abused Children, Gathering Place for Women, Loved Twice, Operation Homefront, Project Night Night, Safe Nest Shelter, Wellspring Family Services
backpacks	Camp To Belong, Standup For Kids, Think Dignity
bags with zippers	Think Dignity
Barbie dolls	Barbie Girls Project
baseball cards	Baseball Almanac, Cards2Kids, Collectibles With Causes
baskets, little plastic mesh berry	California Wildlife Center
bath benches, transfer boards, safety bars, tub transfer benches, commodes	Convalescent Aid Society
bedding: sheets (linens), twin size, mattress protectors, pillows	Animal Rescue, Animal Shelter, Humane Society, Patriots and Paws, Safe Nest Shelter, Sunnyvale Presbyterian Church's Refugee Outreach
beds and mattresses	Donation Town, Spring Back Recycling
beds: hospital, bed rails	Convalescent Aid Society
bicycles	Berkeley Parents Network, Bikes For The World Inc., Bikeworks, Recycle-A-Bike, Sunnyvale Presbyterian Church's Refugee Outreach, Trips For Kids
blankets	Animal Rescue, Animal Shelter, Humane Society, Children's Hunger Fund, Shared Bread, Sunnyvale Presbyterian Church's Refugee Outreach, Think Dignity, Warm Hearts ~ Warm Babies
blankets, handmade	Animal Rescue, Animal Shelter, Humane Society, Children's Hunger Fund, Shared Bread, Standup For Kids, Sunnyvale Presbyterian Church's Refugee Outreach, Think Dignity, Warm Hearts ~ Warm Babies
books and school text-books	Book Aid International, Books For Africa Inc., Got Books?
books: audio	Re-Book It
books: children's books, pregnancy, birth, babies, and parenting	Blossom Birth, Books for Treats, Friends of the Library, International Book Project, Project Night Night, Ronald McDonald House
bookshelves	Free Arts for Abused Children
bras and underwear	Gathering Place for Women, Safe Nest Shelter
brooms	Safe Nest Shelter
building materials: bricks, doors, lumber, windows, ceiling fans	ANEW, Habitat for Humanity
bus passes	Safe Nest Shelter
calendars, planners	Safe Nest Shelter
camera, digital or disposable	Free Arts for Abused Children, Operation Homefront
camera, digital to recycle	EcoPhones
cameras, old	Donation Town, Historic Camera, Kid Camera Project, Naylor Museum of Photographic History, Recycling for Charities
canes, quad canes, crutches, wheelchairs	Church that supports a missionary program, Convalescent Aid Society
cards, greeting	Retirement home
carpet	ANEW

Item	Charity
cars	Children's Hunger Fund
cassettes, audio	Eco Disc
cat litter	Burbank Animal Shelter
CDs and DVDs	GreenDisk, Re-Book It
cell phones to recycle	EcoPhones, Operation Homefront
chairs, folding	Free Arts for Abused Children
cleaning supplies including Lysol spray	Animal Rescue, Animal Shelter, Humane Society, Safe Nest Shelter
clocks: alarm, wall	Safe Nest Shelter, Sunnyvale Presbyterian Church's Refugee Outreach
clothes vintage (1980)	Bank & Vogue, Country Living
clothes/clothing; including belts, blouses, scarves, slacks, slippers	1736 Family Crisis Center Shelter Partnership, Inc., American Kidney Services, Inc., Brothers' Helpers, Children's Hunger Fund, Dress for Success, Harbor Interfaith Shelter, HopeLink, Human Options, Mend, Out of the Closet, Safe Nest Shelter, SHAWL House, Standup For Kids, Think Dignity, Wardrobe for Opportunity
clothes: children's (sizes 8-14), infant's, pull-ups	H&M Clothing Stores, Safe Nest Shelter, San Diego MOM, Wellspring Family Services
clothes: women suits plus-sized (16, 18, 20, 22, 24)	Dress for Success, Rosie's Place, Wardrobe for Opportunity
coats, jackets, ski jackets, sweaters	Dress for Success, One Warm Coat, Safe Nest Shelter, Shared Bread, Think Dignity, Wardrobe for Opportunity
coffee cans, large plastic	California Wildlife Center
coffee makers and coffee seasonings	Safe Nest Shelter
coins	Bust Half Dollar, Coin Group, Coinstar, Collectibles With Causes, Numismatic Bibliomania Society
computers	American Kidney Services, Inc., Computers With Causes, Global Crisis Solution Center, InterConnection.org, Mend, National Cristina Foundation, On It Foundation, Operation Homefront Recycle Computers 4 Cancer,
computers and laptops to recycle; desktop computers, laptop computers, tablets, cell phones, LCD monitors (CRT monitors $10 fee per monitor), keyboards, mice, iPods, MP3 players, printers, printer and copier, toner cartridges, servers, digital cameras, battery back-ups, networking and wireless devices, computer hardware components (including memory modules) cables, software, audio speakers, carts, laptops accessories, modems, bulk wire, used cables, circuit boards, partial computers, or computer parts	ASBA, EcoPhones, Goodwill, March of Dimes, The National Cristina Foundation, StRUT, local city hall for electronics round-up
cosmetics (unopened)	Wardrobe for Opportunity
costumes	community theater, high school drama department
cotton (fabric) anything from snippets to cuttings to fat quarters	Project Linus, Senior Centers, charities that quilt or sew, local schools, camps, theater (or sell on Etsy)
cotton balls	California Wildlife Center
curling irons	Safe Nest Shelter
decorating materials (buttons, feathers, foam, googley eyes, pipe cleaners, pom poms, sequins, wood shapes)	Free Arts for Abused Children
dental equipment and supplies	Mend, South Bay Children's Health Care
dish detergent	Safe Nest Shelter
dresses: bridesmaid, prom and party	Cinderella Dreams, Cinderella Project (The), Cinderella's Closet, Cinderella's Trunk, Dress for Success, Enchanted Closet (The), Fairy Godmother Project, Fairy Godmothers, Fairy Godmothers Inc., Glass Slipper Project (The), Gowns for Girls, Inside the Dream, LA's Prom Closet. My Fairy Godmother, Operation Fairy Dust, Priceless Gown Project, Princess Project (The), Ruby Room (The), Working Wardrobes,

Item	Charity
duct tape	Impact Bay Area
DVD-Rs	Impact Bay Area
DVDs	Blossom Birth, DVDs To The Troops, Re-Book It
electronics, small	ASBA
envelopes, padded DVD	Impact Bay Area
eye glasses	Give the Gift of Sight, Lions Clubs International
fabric notions including thread, trims	Central Christian Church, Mend
fabric, cotton fabric, cotton blends, flannel, fleece	Central Christian Church, Helping Hands Torrance Woman's Club, Project Linus, The Comforters at Westchester Lutheran Church
fans	Sunnyvale Presbyterian Church's Refugee Outreach
feminine hygiene supplies	Children's Hunger Fund, Gathering Place for Women, Shared Bread
food, pantry items and non-perishable foods: beans, canned foods, canned fruit, canned stews/soups, canned tuna or meats, canned vegetables, coffee, cooking oil, cup-o-soups, ketchup, macaroni and cheese, tuna/hamburger helper, ramen noodles, rice, SpaghettiO's®, spaghetti sauce, sugar, tea, pasta, peanut butter	Central Christian Church, Children's Hunger Fund, Gathering Place for Women, Harbor Interfaith Shelter, HopeLink, Mend, Operation Homefront, Ronald McDonald House, San Diego MOM, Shared Bread, Safe Nest Shelter, Standup For Kids, and Postal Carrier Drive in May
foreign coins	UNICEF USA
furniture: baby	San Diego MOM
furniture: household furniture	ANEW, Donation Town, Central Christian Church, Furniture Bank Association of North, Harbor Interfaith Shelter, Operation Homefront, SHAWL House
general donations	Cancer Research, Hope Chest Thrift Store, Society of Saint Vincent de Paul
glue, glitter glue	Children's Hunger Fund, Free Arts for Abused Children
hair	Locks of Love, Matter of Trust
hair products (African-American)	Safe Nest Shelter
hair products; combs, hairbrushes, hairdryers	Safe Nest Shelter
handbag or purses, designer (sell rather than donate)	Rebagg
handbags	Dress for Success, Wardrobe for Opportunity
hangers	local dry cleaner
hardware	ANEW
hearing aids	Lion Clubs
helmets	Sunnyvale Presbyterian Church's Refugee Outreach
household furnishings and items	1736 Family Crisis Center Shelter Partnership, Inc., Mend, Patriots and Paws, San Diego MOM
ink jet cartridges and toner cartridges to recycle	EcoPhones, Operation Homefront
iPod and iPod speakers	Free Arts for Abused Children
IV poles	Convalescent Aid Society
jewelry making materials (fancy beads, fasteners, wire)	Free Arts for Abused Children
jewelry, costume jewelry	Dress for Success, Wardrobe for Opportunity, Working Wardrobes
kitchen garbage bags	Impact Bay Area
kitchen supplies, bowls, cooking utensils, cutlery, dining tables, dishes, kitchen tables and chairs small, pots, pans, plates, toasters, wooden forks and spoons	Free Arts for Abused Children, Patriots and Paws, Safe Nest Shelter, Sunnyvale Presbyterian Church's Refugee Outreach
knickknacks	Excess Access
lamps	Sunnyvale Presbyterian Church's Refugee Outreach
latex gloves	California Wildlife Center
LP records	Re-Book It
magazines	Retirement home
maternity clothes	Blossom Birth

Item	Charity
medical supplies: cold tablets and pain relievers (adult)	Safe Nest Shelter
medical supplies; children cold tablets, children pain relievers, ear thermometers	Mend, Safe Nest Shelter
musical instruments	Local public school music teachers, local music store, local Boy Scout or Girl Scout Council, Dreaming Zebra Foundation, Operation Happy Note, The Salvation Army
National Geographic magazines	Books For Soldiers. Bridge to Asia, Darien Book Aid Plan Inc.
office supplies including name tags	Impact Bay Area, Mend
Oriental Rugs	Weaving Art Museum & Research Institute
paper products	Ronald McDonald House, Safe Nest Shelter
paper: notebooks (paper), sketch books, stationary	Children's Hunger Fund, Free Arts for Abused Children, Safe Nest Shelter
paper: watercolor, vellum drawing, colored, construction, copier	Children's Hunger Fund, Free Arts for Abused Children, Healing Tree Arts, Impact Bay Area
peanuts (packing)	Most pack and ship places will take them
pencils	Children's Hunger Fund
pens, Sharpies	Children's Hunger Fund, Free Arts for Abused Children
personal care items	Standup For Kids
pet hair	Matter of Trust
pet supplies and pet grooming supplies	Animal hospitals, animal shelters, Burbank Animal Shelter, kennels, Patriots and Paws, Veterinarians
pets: canned cat and dog food, pet food	California Wildlife Center, Burbank Animal Shelter
pictures	Historic Camera
pop tabs (pull tabs)	Ronald McDonald House
postage stamps (postcard and first-class)	Free Arts for Abused Children, Safe Nest Shelter
poster board	Free Arts for Abused Children
printer, photo	Free Arts for Abused Children
robes	Safe Nest Shelter
sandpaper	Free Arts for Abused Children
school supplies, rulers	Children's Hunger Fund, Gathering Place for Women, Operation Homefront, Safe Nest Shelter
Sharpie markers (see also pens)	Free Arts for Abused Children
shelving	Free Arts for Abused Children
shoes	Mend, Wellspring Family Services
shoes: men's	Dress for Success, Think Dignity, Mend, Wardrobe for Opportunity. Working Wardrobes
sleeping bags	Camp To Belong, Standup For Kids, Think Dignity
sneakers	Nike Reuse-a-Shoe
socks, children's	Gathering Place for Women, Think Dignity,
sofas	Patriots and Paws
sports equipment: golf, baseball, hockey, snow sports, lacrosse	Boys & Girls club, Children's Hunger Fund, Clubs-fore-Kids PGA, Gift of Sports Foundation Inc., Play It Again Sports, police athletic league, school programs, youth centers
staplers	Children's Hunger Fund
storage containers with lids (plastic clear 16"w x 12"l x 12"h); storage bins (plastic 5 to 12 gallon)	Free Arts for Abused Children, Safe Nest Shelter
stuffed animals, small, plush	Children's Hunger Fund, Los Angeles County Toy Loan Program, Our Lady of Hope Resident, Project Night Night, SAFE
suits: men big and tall	Rosie's Place, Think Dignity, Wardrobe for Opportunity,
suits: women's and men's business	Dress for Success, Tailored For Success, Inc.
supplies	San Diego MOM
survival items	Children's Hunger Fund
sweatpants and sweatshirts	Think Dignity
sweatshirts sleeves (for possums to burrow in)	California Wildlife Center
table cloths, plastic	Free Arts for Abused Children
television to recycle	ASBA
throw rugs (large)	Safe Nest Shelter

Item	Charity
tickets to local children's activities	Mend
tissue	Impact Bay Area, Safe Nest Shelter
toilet paper	Free Arts for Abused Children, Safe Nest Shelter
toiletries: soap (liquid hand, bar, little soaps), shampoo (little), conditioner (mini conditioners) toothpaste, deodorant (antiperspirant, deodorant), razor (disposable)	Brothers' Helpers, Children's Hunger Fund, Gathering Place for Women, Impact Bay Area, Safe Nest Shelter, Think Dignity, women's shelters,
towels: paper, bath, dish	Animal rescue, animal shelter, California Wildlife Center, Free Arts for Abused Children Humane Society, Impact Bay Area, Sunnyvale Presbyterian Church's Refugee Outreach
toys, boys	1736 Family Crisis Center Shelter Partnership, Inc., Children's Hunger Fund, Safe Nest Shelter
toys; balls, beach toys, jump ropes, sidewalk chalk	Gleaning for the World, Los Angeles County Toy Loan Program, Mend, Wellspring Family Services
treasure boxes (small boxes with lids that fit over the entire box)	Free Arts for Abused Children
t-shirts	Animal rescue, animal shelter, humane society
umbrellas and rain gear	Think Dignity, Wardrobe for Opportunity
vacuum cleaners	Safe Nest Shelter
vases: clean ones	local hospital gift store or florist
VHS tapes, blank	Impact Bay Area
video games	Friends of the Library
videos, children	Friends of the Library, Ronald McDonald House
wedding gown	Brides Against Breast Cancer®, Making Memories
yarn, acrylic	Project Linus

1736 Family Crisis Center Shelter Ptr 323-737-3900
2116 Arlington Ave Ste 200 Los Angeles CA 90018
501(c)3 95-3989251
www.1736familycrisiscenter.org
Clothes, household items, and toys.

American Kidney Services, Inc. 770-872-4260
6200 Ross Rd Doraville GA 30340-3112
501(c)3 20-2504107
www.akspickup.org/donate_vintage.html
Clothes, and computers.

Animal Rescue, Animal Hospital, Animal Shelter, Humane Society, Kennels, Veterinarians
Multiple locations nationwide
Search Google for Web sites and specific information.
Blankets, cleaning supplies, towels, sheets, and t-shirts.

Arizona Small Business Association (ASBA) 602-306-4000
4600 E Washington St Ste 340 Phoenix AZ 85034
501(c)3 94-2383015
www.asba.com
Appliances, computers, TV's, small electronics, anything with a cord.

Asset Network for Education Worldwide (ANEW)   213-943-4400
3150 N San Fernando Rd Ste 117 Los Angeles CA 90065-1413
501(c)3 20-3884159
www.anewfound.org
Carpet, ceiling fans, doors, hardware, and all furniture.

Baby2Baby 323-933-2229
6435 Wilshire Blvd Los Angeles 90048-4907
501(c)3 46-4503539
www.baby2baby.org
Baby clothes.

Bank & Vogue .... 613-747-8465 x 178
1195 Michael St Ottawa, Ontario, K1J 72T
www.bankvogue.com/vintage-clothing/
Vintage clothes (1980).

Barbie Girls Project (The) 317-493-2227
www.facebook.com/pages/The-Barbie-Girls-Project/135528563210747
Barbie dolls.

Baseball Almanac
8263 SW 107th Avenue, Apt A Miami, FL 33173
www.baseball-almanac.com/support.shtml
Baseball cards.

Berkeley Parents Network
2930 Domingo Street Suite 17 Berkeley CA 94705-2454
501(c)3 46-4347971
http://parents.berkeley.edu/recommend/charity/bikes.html
Bicycles.

Bikes For The World Inc............................. 703-740-7856
1408 N Fillmore St Ste 11 Arlington VA 22201-3819
501(c)3 27-5426399
www.bikesfortheworld.org
Bicycles.

Bikeworks 206-725-9408
3715 S Hudson St Seattle, WA 98118
501(c)3 91-1753062
www.bikeworks.org/donations.php
Bicycles.

Blossom Birth..650-321-2326
505 Barron Ave Palo Alto CA 94306
501(c)3 77-0506942
www.blossombirth.org or http://BlossomBirthCenter.com
Baby care items, books (pregnancy, birth, babies, and parenting) in other languages, baby clothes, DVDs, maternity clothes and children's items.

Book Aid International................................44 (0) 20 7733 3577
39 — 41 Coldharbour Lane, Camberwell London SE5 9NR UK
www.bookaid.org
Books and school text-books.

Books For Africa Inc.
26 Exchange St E Ste 411 Saint Paul, MN 55101-2264
501(c)3 41-1627391
www.booksforafrica.org
Books and school text-books.

Books For Soldiers
c/o Storm Williams 21370 SW Langer Farms Pkwy Ste 142, Box 123 Sherwood, OR 97140
501(c)3 operated by Red Grail Ministries
www.BooksForSoldiers.com
National Geographic magazines, and books.

Books for Treats..408-998-7977
1440 Newport Ave San Jose CA
501(c)3 45-4888768
www.booksfortreats.org
Children's books.

Boy & Girls Clubs of America 404-487-5700
1275 Peachtree Street NE Atlanta GA 30309-3506
501(c)3 13-5562976
www.bgca.org
Sports equipment: golf, baseball, hockey, snow sports, lacrosse.Multiple locations nationwide.

Brides Against Breast Cancer 404-698-1000
3308 Laventure Dr Ste B170 Atlanta GA 30341
501(c)3 donation letter after donating
www.bridesagainstbreastcancer.org
Wedding gown.

Bridge to Asia 510-665-3998
1505 Juanita Way Berkeley CA 94702-1103
501(c)3 94-3055124
www.bridge.org
Books, encyclopedias, dictionaries, almanacs, and atlases.

Brothers' Helpers 818-949-4338
215 Foothill Blvd La Canada CA 91011
501(c)3 20-5806537
www.BrothersHelpers.org
Basic toiletries, clothing, shampoo, and toothpaste.

Burbank Animal Shelter 818-238-3344
1150 North Victory Pl Burbank CA 91502
501(c)3 95-4469452
http://thevbas.org
Cat litter, pet food, and pet grooming supplies.

Bust Half Dollar
www.BustHalfPrices.com/bhnc.php
Coins.

California Wildlife Center 818-222-2685
PO Box 2022 Malibu CA 90265
501(c)3 95-4580790
www.cawildlife.org
Canned cat and dog food, cotton balls, coffee cans (large plastic), latex gloves, mesh berry baskets (little plastic), sweatshirts sleeves (for possums to burrow in), and towels.

Camp To Belong 774-258-0269
PO Box 1147 Victor ID 83455
501(c)3 94-3229145
www.CampToBelong.org
Art supplies, backpacks, and sleeping bags.

Cancer Research 800-443-4224
Multiple locations nationwide
Search Google for Web sites and specific information
General donations will pick up. Multiple locations nationwide

Cards2Kids..312-362-2452
141 W Jackson Blvd Ste 500 Chicago, IL 60604
www.cards2kids.org
Baseball cards.

Central Christian Church 702-735-4004
1001 New Beginnings Dr Henderson NV 89011
501(c)3 55-0385729
www.centralonline.tv
Food, furniture, material (fabric), notions, and thread.

Children's Hunger Fund............................800-708-7589
13931 Balboa Blvd Sylmar CA 91342
501(c)3 95-4335462
www.chfus.org
Bar soaps, beans, blankets, cars, clothing, feminine products, glue, notebooks, paper, pencils, pens, stuffed animals, rice, rulers, school supplies, shampoo, soap, sports equipment, staplers, survival items, toothpaste, and toys for boys.

Church that supports a missionary program
Multiple locations nationwide
Search Google for Web sites and specific information
Walkers and wheelchairs.

Cinderella Dreams, Cinderella Project (The), Cinderella's Closet, Cinderella's Trunk, Dress for Success, Enchanted Closet (The), Fairy Godmother Project, Fairy Godmothers, Fairy Godmothers

Inc., Glass Slipper Project (The), Gowns for Girls, Inside the Dream, My Fairy Godmother, Operation Fairy Dust, Priceless Gown Project, Princess Project (The), Ruby Room (The)
Multiple locations nationwide
Search Google for Web sites and specific information
Bridesmaid and prom dresses.

Clubs-fore-Kids (PGA) ....561-624-8400 ask to be transferred to Section Level
100 Avenue of the Champions Palm Beach Gardens FL 33418
Golf clubs. Contact golf course's pro shop.

Coin Group (The)....................................233 244 22 52 39
PO Box OS 2360 OSU Accra / Ghana
http://www.coingroup.org/donate-your-coins/%20Ghana
Coins.

Coinstar..800-928-2274
1800 114th Avenue SE Bellevue, WA 98004
www.coinstar.com/donatecharity
Coins.

Collectibles With Causes 888-228-7320
501(c)3 46-1883892
www.collectibleswithcauses.org/donate-art.html
Art work, baseball cards, and coins.

Comforters (The) at Westchester Lutheran Church   310-670-5422
7831 S Sepulveda Blvd Los Angeles, CA 90045
www.wlcs.org/comforters
fabric: not particular about how they get the fabric or what type of fabrics.

Computers With Causes............................888-228-7320
6900 Westcliff Dr Ste 506 Las Vegas, NV 89145-0198
www.computerswithcauses.org
Computers.

Convalescent Aid Society (CAS) 626-793-1696
3255 East Foothill Blvd Pasadena CA 91107
501(c)3 95-1782304
https://www.convalescentaidsociety.com/
Bath benches, hospital beds, canes, commodes, crutches, IV poles, quad canes, bed rails, safety bars, tub transfer benches, transfer boards, walkers, and wheelchairs.

Country Living
www.countryliving.com/antiques
Vintage clothes (1980).

Darien Book Aid Plan Inc. 203-655-2777
1926 Post Rd Darien CT 06820
501(c)3 06-6041210
www.DarienBookAid.org
National Geographic magazines, and books.

Donation Town
multiple locations nationwide

www.donationtown.org or www.donationtown.org/donation-pick-up.html
Baby clothes, cameras, Furniture, video games, beds and mattresses. Inform them when it was used around a smoker or pets as people in fragile health can be extremely sensitive to cigarette smoke or pet hair. Coit Carpet Cleaning company cleans mattress with a dry process if you want to clean a mattress.

Dreaming Zebra Foundation (The) 503-206-6400
5331 SW Macadam Ave Ste 285 Portland OR 97239-3849
501(c)3 26-2326071
www.dreamingzebra.org
Musical instruments.

Dress for Success Worldwide 212-532-1922
32 East 31st St 7th Floor New York NY 10016
501(c)3 13-4040377
www.dressforsuccess.org/news_media_pr_SOS2007.aspx
Cleaned items on hangers (styles less than five years old): blouses, costume jewelry, handbags, jackets, scarves, shoes, slacks, and suits.

DVDs To The Troops
www.dvdstothetroops.org
DVDs

Eco Disk... 253-471-1800
2514 92nd St S Lakewood WA 98499-9377
www.ecodisk.com
Recycles all audio cassette tapes.

EcoPhones 888-326-7466
4254 Simonton Rd Dallas TX 75220
www.ecophones.com
Recycling cell phones, digital cameras, ink jet cartridges and laptop computers. Free shipping.

Excess Access... 415-242-6041
99 St Germain Ave San Francisco CA 94114
www.Excessaccess.com
Excess Access Random knickknacks. Got something you don't know what to do with? Match your items with nonprofit wish lists.

Free Arts for Abused Children 310-313-4278
11099 S La Cienega Blvd Ste 235 Los Angeles CA 90045
501(c)3 95-3252001
www.freearts.org
Acrylic paint (water based, 1/2 gallon bottles or larger), baby wipes, bookshelves, canvases, storage containers with lids (clear plastic 16"w x 12"l x 12"h), construction paper, copier paper, decorating materials (buttons, feathers, foam, googley eyes, pipe cleaners, pom poms, sequins, wood shapes), digital camera, disposable cameras, folding chairs, glitter glue, glitter paint, gray sculpting clay, iPod, iPod speakers, jewelry making materials (including fancy beads, fasteners, and wire), paper towels, photo printer, plastic table cloths, postage stamps (33¢ and 46¢), poster board, sandpaper, Sharpie brand markers, shelving, sketch books, tempera paint, toilet paper, treasure boxes (small boxes with lids that fit over the entire box), vellum drawing paper, watercolor paper, wooden forks, and wooden spoons.

Friends of the Library
local library
Search Google for Web sites and specific information
Books, and video games.

Furniture Bank Association of North America 916-635-0664
Furniture for Families
PO Box 34 Folsom, CA 95763
501(c)3 54-2115344
www.furniturebanks.org
Furniture.

Gathering Place for Women 303-321-4198
1535 High St Denver CO 80218
501(c)3 84-1021059
www.tgpdenver.org
Non-perishable food: baby food, beans, canned fruit, canned stews/soups, canned tuna or meats, canned vegetables, coffee, cup-o-soups, pasta, peanut butter, powdered Similac formula, ramen noodles, rice, SpaghettiOs, spaghetti sauce, tea, and tuna/hamburger helper. Toiletries: antiperspirant, baby formula, baby lotion, baby shampoo, baby soap, baby wipes, children's socks, conditioner, deodorant, diaper cream, diapers, disposable razors, feminine hygiene supplies, formula, pedialyte, shampoo, sippy cups, soap, toothpaste, and underwear. Storage bins, (plastic 5 to 12 gallon) and school supplies.

Gift of Sports Foundation Inc......................949-388-2359
3940 Guava Dr Naples FL 34104-4469
501(c)3 47-3909100
www.sportsgift.org
Sports equipment.

Give the Gift of Sight 888-935-4589
4000 Luxottica Pl Mason OH 45040
www.givethegiftofsight.org/gosagency
Eye glasses. Drop off at LensCrafters, Pearle Vision, Sears Optical, Sunglass Hut, or Target Optical.

Gleaning for the World
Attention: Teddy Bear Brigade
7539 Stage Rd; PO Box 645 Concord, VA 24538
501(c)3 54-1930105
Toys.

Global Crisis Solution Center
links to other websites
www.globalcrisis.info/computerrecycle.html
Computers.

Got Books?..978-416-8288
Big Hearted Books & Clothing Inc.
5 Merchant St. Unit B Sharon MA, 02067
www.gotbooks.com
School text-books.

GreenDisk 800-305-3475
www.greendisk.com
CDs and DVDs.

H&M Clothing Stores
Sweden
www.hm.com/us
Children's clothes.

Habitat for Humanity of Greater LA 310-323-4663
8739 Artesia Blvd Bellflower CA 90706
501(c)3 33-0416470
www.habitatla.org
Building materials in good, reusable condition: bricks, doors, lumber, and windows. Will pick up. Furniture.

Harbor Interfaith Shelter 310-831-0603
670 W 9th St San Pedro CA 90731
501(c)3 33-0031099
www.harborinterfaith.org
Appliances, clothing, food, and household furniture.

Helping Hands
Torrance Woman's Club 310-375-6926
1422 Engracia Ave Torrance, CA 90501
501(c)3 33-0249000
www.torrancewomansclub.org
Cotton fabric, cotton blends, flannel, but not wool, silk, or polyester.

Historic Camera
http://historiccamera.com
Cameras, and pictures.

Hope Chest Thrift Store 626-579-3403
4203 N Peck Road El Monte CA 91732
501(c)3 95-2287909
General donations.

HopeLink 702-566-0576
178 Westminster Way Henderson NV 89015
501(c)3 94-3202139
www.link2hope.org
Non-perishable goods and clothing.

Human Options... 949-737-5242
5540 Trabuco Rd Ste 100 Irvine CA 92620
501(c)3 95-3667817
www.HumanOptions.org
Clothing for their store Classy Second.

Impact Bay Area.. 510-208-0474
PO Box 23831 Oakland CA 94623
501(c)3 943123451
www.impactbayarea.org
Blank VHS tapes, boxes of tissue, colored paper, duct tape, DVD-Rs, kitchen garbage bags, liquid hand soap, name tags, padded DVD envelopes, and paper towels.

InterConnection.org 866-621-1068
3415 Stone Way N Seattle, WA, 98103
501(c)3 93-1262843
www.interconnection.org
Computers.

International Book Project 859-254-6771
1440 Delaware Ave Lexington KY 40505
501(c)3 61-6039627
Books. Does not accept: books in poor condition (torn, missing pages), encyclopedias, magazines, textbooks copyrighted before 2000.

Kid Camera Project
1401 Frederica St Owensboro KY 42301-4804
501(c)3 27-3135298
www.kidcameraproject.org
Cameras.

Lions Clubs Int'l Health and Children's Services   630-571-5466
300 W 22nd St Oak Brook IL 60523-8842
http://www.lionsclubs.org/EN/how-we-serve/health/sight/eyeglass-recycling.php
Eye glasses. Multiple locations nationwide.

Local library
Local libraries may have preferences of what they wish to receive. Call the library (especially Friends of the Library) and ask what they are looking for. If they aren't interested, ask for a suggestion in your area where you could donate your books (a school, a senior community, Rotary/Kiwanis club, etc.).

Locks of Love 888-896-1588
234 Southern Blvd W Palm Beach FL 33405-2701
501(c)3 65-0755522
www.locksoflove.org
Hair. Donating your hair could help clean up future oil spills.

Los Angeles County Toy Loan Program ...213-744-4344
501(c)3 95-6095645
http://www.ladpss.org/dpss/toyloan/default.cfm
Books, toys and stuffed animal.

Loved Twice..................................510-652-2229
4123 Broadway Ste 815 Oakland, CA 94611
501(c)3 94-3441434
http://lovedtwice.org
Baby clothes to one year old.

Matter of Trust 415-242-6041
99 Saint Germain Ave San Francisco, CA 94114
501(c)3 06-1530091
www.matteroftrust.org
Hair. Collects human and pet hair to create booms that soak up oil.

Mend..................................818-897-2443
10641 N San Fernando Rd Pacoima CA 91331
501(c)3 237306337
www.mendpoverty.org
Clothes, computers, medical supplies, shoes, food, clothing, household items, new shoes (all in good condition) office supplies, dental supplies, medical supplies (NO medicines of any kind accepted), new toys, tickets to local children's activities, new fabric, trims and threads, arts and crafts supplies for after school children.

National Council of Jewish Women 800-400-6259
Multiple locations nationwide
www.ncjwla.org

National Cristina Foundation....................203-863-9100
339 Lea Dr West Chester PA 19382
501(c)3 06-1157227
www.cristina.org
Computers.

National Furniture Bank Association........614-545-3845
118 S Yale Ave Columbus OH 43222-1369
www.furniturebanks.org
Furniture. Multiple locations nationwide

Naylor Museum of Photographic History . 617-731-6603
102 Fernwood Rd Chestnut Hill MA 02467-2907
Cameras

Nike Reuse-a-Shoe 800-352-6453
3552 Avenue of Commerce Memphis TN 38125
http://www.active.com/running/articles/2-ways-to-recycle-your-running-shoes
Sneakers (any brand). Multiple locations nationwide

Numismatic Bibliomania Society (The)
www.CoinBooks.org
Coins.

On It Foundation (Opportunities Necessary to Increase Technology) 305-244-6454
18520 NW 67th Ave Ste 186 Miami FL 33015
www.theonitfoundation.org
Computer equipment.

One Warm Coat.. 877-663-9276
2443 Fillmore St #380-5363 San Francisco CA 94115
501(c)3 74-3045243
www.onewarmcoat.org
Coats, ski jackets, and sweaters.

Operation Happy Note............................. 320-759-9003
518 Hawthorne St Alexandria MN 56308
https://www.facebook.com/O.H.N.Official/
Musical instruments.

Operation Homefront............................... 210-659-7756
1355 Central Parkway S Ste 100 San Antonio TX 78232
501(c)3 320033325
www.operationhomefront.net/socal
Baby items, computers (Pentium III or higher, 650 MHZ), digital cameras, e-trash recycling (cell phones, ink cartridges, toner), furniture, non-perishable foods, and school supplies.

Our Lady of Hope Residence.................... 518-785-4551
Little Sisters of the Poor
1 Jeanne Jugan Ln Latham NY 12110
http://littlesistersofthepoorlatham.org
Small stuffed animals. Contact: Sister Frances

Out of the Closet 877-274-2548
20084 Cherokee Station New York NY 10075-0000
501(c)3 13-3521018
http://outofthecloset.org/
Clothes.

PaperBackSwap 678-802-1922
3651 Peachtree Parkway Suite E-390 Suwanee, GA 30024
www.PaperBackSwap.com
Books.

Patriots and Paws 714-323-7229
9121 Atlanta Ave #471 Huntington Beach CA 92646
501(c)3 38-3852940
http://www.patriotsandpaws.org/
Dishes, bedding, sofas, dining tables, home furnishings, appliances, kitchenware, and pet related items.

Play It Again Sports 763-520-8480
605 US-169 #400 Minneapolis MN 55441
www.playitagainsports.com
Sports equipment (golf, baseball, hockey, snow sports, and lacrosse). You can sell or donate. Multiple locations nationwide.

Project Linus 309-585-0686
PO Box 1548 Belton MO 64012-1108
501(c)3 84-1362696
www.projectlinus.org
Acrylic yarn, cotton, flannel fabric, fleece, or make a blanket.

Project Night Night....................................415-310-0360
148 Beulah St San Francisco CA 94117
501(c)3 20-2877016
www.projectnightnight.com
Baby blankets, children's books and stuffed animals.

Rebagg 844-373-7723
West 37th St New York City NY 10018
https://rebagg.com/
Designer purses (sell rather than donate)

Re-Book It 877-877-4080
The Last Bookstore
453 S Spring St Los Angeles, CA 90013
501(c)3 provided by partner
http://rebookit.org
Books, CDs, DVDs, audio books, and LP records. Service area: Los Angeles, San Bernardino, Ventura, and Riverside.

Recycle Computers 4 Cancer 781-789-5413
70 Heritage Way Hanover MA 02339
501(c)3 42-1705825
www.recyclecomputers4cancer.org
Computers.

Recycle-A-Bike..401-525-1822
12 Library Ct Providence RI 02909-3403
501(c)3 27-1157693
www.recycleabike.org
Bicycles.

Recycling for Charities............................ 866-630-7557
8025 S Good Harbor Trl Cedar MI 49621-8574
501(c)3 26-1874193
www.recyclingforcharities.com
Cameras.

Retirement Home
Multiple locations nationwide
Search Google for Web sites and specific information
Magazines and greeting cards for craft activities.

Ronald McDonald House Charities of Southern CA   626-585-1588
763 S Pasadena Ave Pasadena CA 91105
501(c)3 95-3167869
www.pasadenarmh.org
Children's books, pantry items, paper products, and pop tabs from cans.

Rosie's Place.. 617-442-9322
889 Harrison Ave Roxbury MA 02118
501(c)3 84-1703424
www.rosies.org
Plus size women's suits (16, 18, 20, 22, and 24).

SAFE (Stuffed Animals for Emergencies) 937-708-0251
PO Box 119 Orient OH 43146
501(c)3 45-5062724
www.stuffedanimalsforemergencies.org
Stuffed animals.

Safe Nest 702-877-0133
2915 W Charleston Blvd Ste 12 Las Vegas NV 89102
501(c)3 94-2411883
www.safenest.org
African-American hair products, alarm clocks, aluminum foil, baby shampoo, bedding, bottle brushes (baby), bottles, bras, broom, bus passes, calendars and planners, canned fruit, cereal, children and adult cold tablets, children and adult pain relievers, children books, children's clothing (sizes 8-14), children's shoes, coats and jackets, coffee maker, coffee seasonings, cooking oil, curling irons, deodorant, diaper wipes, diapers, dish detergent, ear thermometers, Enfamil with iron, food containers, food storage bags (all sizes), hair products, hairbrushes and combs, hairdryers, ketchup, Kleenex, Lysol spray, macaroni and cheese, pacifiers, paper goods, pillow and mattress protector, pots and pans, pull-ups, robes, scarves, school supplies, silverware, Spaghetti O's, stamps, stationary, sugar, throw rug (large), toaster, toilet paper, toothpaste, toys, underwear, vacuum cleaner.

Salvation Army (The)
contact your local Salvation Army—not necessarily the donation center.
Musical Instruments. They have an extensive musical program teaching officers and children how to play.

San Diego MOM [Military Outreach Ministries]   619-461-4164
4426 Harbinson Ave La Mesa CA 91942
501(c)3 76-0817487
http://sandiegomom.org/

Household items, infant or children's clothes and supplies, baby furniture and food.

Shared Bread..................................310-372-8445
243 S Broadway Redondo Beach CA 90277
http://fumcrb.org/bread
Blankets, canned foods, hygiene items, and jackets.

SHAWL House
(Support for Harbor Area Women's Lives)310-521-9310
936 S Center St San Pedro CA 90732
www.shawlwomenshouse.org
Clothing and furniture.

Sisters of Charity of Rolling Hills 310-831-4104
28600 Palos Verdes Dr E Rancho Palos Verdes CA 90275
501(c)3 956123759
https://www.facebook.com/Sisters-of-Charity-of-Rolling-Hills-189660803438/
Clothing and furniture and everything.

Society of Saint Vincent de Paul 314-576-3993
58 Progress Parkway Maryland Heights MO 63043-3706
501(c)3 48-0910393
http://svdpusa.org/
General donations.

South Bay Children's Health Care.............310-316-1212
410 S Camino Real Redondo Beach CA 90277
www.sbchc.com
Dental equipment and supplies.

Spring Back Recycling
6333 Noel Dr Brentwood TN 37027-4841
501(c)3 27-5539358
http://springbackrecycling.com/
Beds and mattresses.

Standup For Kids 800-365-4543
83 Walton St Ste 500 Atlanta GA 30303
501(c)3 33-0414855
www.standupforkids.org
Backpacks, blankets, clothing, food, personal care items, and sleeping bags.

STudents Recycling Used Technology (STRUT)541-296-2630
3855 Fifteen Mile Rd The Dalles OR 97058
www.strut.org
Desktop computers, laptop computers, tablets, cell phones, LCD monitors (CRT monitors $10 fee per monitor), keyboards, mice, iPods, MP3 players, printers, printer and copier, toner cartridges, servers, digital cameras, battery back-ups, networking and wireless devices, computer hardware components (including memory modules) cables, software, audio speakers, carts, laptops accessories, modems, bulk wire, used cables, circuit boards, partial computers, or computer parts.

Tailored For Success, Inc............................781-324-0499
587 Pleasant St Malden MA 02148
501(c)3 04-3488106

www.tailoredforsuccess.org
Cleaned items on hangers: women's and men's business suits.

Think Dignity 619-537-8736
1228 University Ave #200-5 San Diego CA 92103
501(c)3 33-1146733
www.thinkdignity.org
Backpacks, bags with zippers, blankets, coats, deodorant, large sized clothes (men's and women's XL or above), mini conditioners, mini shampoo, rain gear, shampoos, shaving items, shoes, sleeping bags, soaps, socks, sweatpants, sweatshirts, toiletries, toothbrushes, toothpaste, umbrellas, and warm clothing.

Trips For Kids 415-458-2986
610 4th St San Rafael CA 94901-3211
501(c)3 68-0159458
www.tripsforkids.org/
Bicycles.

UNICEF USA... 800-367-5437
Attention: Change for Good Program
125 Maiden Lane New York NY 10038
501(c)3 13-1760110
www.unicefusa.org/campaigns/changeforgood/.
Foreign coins.

Wardrobe for Opportunity........................... 510-463-4100
570 14th St Ste 5 Oakland CA 94612
501(c)3 68-0369734
www.wardrobe.org
Clean clothing on hangers: belts, coats, handbags, jewelry, plus-sized suits for women, and big and tall suits for men, shoes, umbrellas, and unopened cosmetics.

Warm Hearts ~ Warm Babies..................... 303-975-6394
PO Box 830 Arvada CO 80001
501(c)3 31-1728454
www.warmheartswarmbabies.org
Crochet, knit, quilt, or sew for infants.

Weaving Art Museum & Research Institute
217 Thompson St New York NY 10012-1361
501(c)3 94-3269631
Oriental Rugs.

Wellspring Family Services 206-902-4233
1900 Rainier Ave S Seattle WA 98144-4606
501(c)3 91-0567261
https://www.wellspringfs.org/get-involved/donate-clothing-other-essentials
Shoes, socks, balls, jump ropes, beach toys, sidewalk chalk, diapers wipes, infant formula, clothes 0-17.

Working Wardrobes.................................... 714-210-2460
1851 Kettering St Irvine CA 92614
501(c)3 33-0669145
www.WorkingWardrobes.org
Jewelry, men's shoes, party dresses, and prom dresses.

World Craniofacial Foundation.................972-566-6669   www.worldcf.org
7777 Forest Ln Ste C-616 Dallas TX 75230   Airline miles.
501(c)3 75-2304155

IRS DEDUCTION

To help soften the blow that you didn't make any money by selling your stuff, I've outlined the IRS rules so that you can take advantage of your charitable nature.

There is a book called *Money For Your Used Clothing* (www.MFYUC.com) that may help you when you are donating a large amount of clothes. The book is a form where you check off the number of sweaters that are in good or fair (I don't remember what the categories names are) condition. Then, it has a fair market value for those pieces for clothing and similar common household items.

Good Household Goods

Many charities are happy to accept used clothing and household goods.

Be sure that it is a charity. Some of the suggestions that I have made are organizations or good causes but not a charity by IRS terms. Check that it has the 501(c)3 status. Check out the IRS's online list (Publication 78) of exempt organizations or call the IRS toll free at 877-829-5500 and ask about the group's tax status. www.irs.gov/Charities-&-Non-Profits/Search-for-Charities

To be deductible, contributions must be made to qualified organizations.

When you give goods, **charities typically provide** a receipt to help support itemized claims. Those receipts will help you meet an IRS requirement that requires you be able to document every gift, regardless of amount. With these donations, if the IRS asks, you must show an official record, such as a written statement from the charity showing the organization's name and the date and amount of the contribution.

The receipts from the charity for your donated goods are for your personal records. The receipt will help you prove that you did indeed donate the property if the IRS asks.

It's up to you—not the IRS, not the charity—to assign a precise value to your donation. The nonprofit won't put a dollar value on this receipt.

The items need to be in good or better condition. The IRS has rules on how to decide what a donated item is worth: claim its fair-market value, or what a willing buyer would pay for that item in its current shape—not what it was worth when it was new.

There are several computer software programs available to help you figure the tax value of your goodwill. Bankrate has some work sheets to help you figure the appropriate amount. www.bankrate.com/finance/money-guides/tax-guide-for-donated-goods.aspx. Many people still prefer to use pen and paper, jotting down the item and its worth as they are pulling it from the closet or dresser drawer. You may want to take a picture of your items at the time when you are donating the items as additional documentation.

It indicates fair market value for some common items as suggested in The Salvation Army's valuation guide. http://satruck.org/donation-value-guide

Charitable contributions only help you at tax-filing time when you itemize deductions. That means you have to keep track of what you give and file the long Form 1040 and Schedule A.

The IRS can deny deductions for items that are deemed of "minimal monetary value." When your total amount of donated articles—or as the IRS calls them, noncash gifts—exceeds $500, you have to file with your tax return Form 8283, Noncash Charitable Contributions, detailing your generosity.

If your donation is more than $500 worth of goods to charity, you must detail your generosity and include it with your tax return Form 8283 Noncash Charitable Contributions [www.irs.gov/pub/irs-pdf/f8283.pdf]. If you don't include the form, the IRS could disallow your claim.

When you claim a deduction of more than $5,000 for **an item**, you must have a qualified **appraiser** provide the value and then attach an appraisal summary (Section B of Form 8283) to your tax return.

You don't have to send in your list of donated items with your return. Simply keep the information with your personal tax records and put the total contribution amount on your Schedule A.

WRAP UP

In the Spring 2012 Getting Organized Magazine article *Clutter Acts Like A Crutch for Many of Us,* Leo Babauto talks about why we hold onto thing (security, self-image, memories, etc.).

As Chapter 2 list delineates, when we sit down and look at what collections we may have, the endless possibilities are staggering. More than we imagined. Perhaps moving beyond a crutch to inhibiting our lives. If you have watched the television show *Hoarders,* you may have seen how trash has buried people. It starts out as a good idea (I can use this for a craft project) and then becomes "there are more projects than there is time!"

Being able to find *Cash From Our Clutter* is a challenging, frustrating and rewarding journey.

Now go through your house and see how many more things are around that you can sell that you didn't know that you could sell. And may you have great success!

Index

C

D

Y

Rounds Miller
AND ASSOCIATES

6318 Ridgepath Court
Rancho Palos Verdes, CA 90275-3248
310.544.9502
www.RoundsMiller.com

Business, Technology and Organizing Training Specialists

PRODUCT CATALOG

Audio/Video Conversion Suite CD

Contains Pix Converter - Pixel reduction Software; Free Studio – convert audio to MP3 and video to MPeg4 - Audacity – Record and Edit Audio - CamStudio – On-Screen Recorder - Wine Bottler – Allows Windows Software to Run on Macintosh

Data CD⁺   **$24.95**

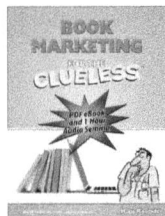

Book Marketing for the Clueless®

Want to sell your books, CDs and DVDs for a profit? This audio/PDF CD includes databases of over 500 catalogs and outlets that market books and instructions on how to solicit your publications including how to be listed with Amazon.com for free.

Audio/Data CD⁺ ISBN 978-1-891440-49-6   **$24.95**
eBook* ISBN 978-1-891440-94-6   **$9.95**

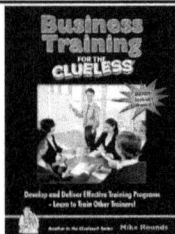

Business Training for the Clueless®

A complete course about becoming a six figure a year business trainer. Contains a complete PDF manual, workbook, training aids, exercise, games, on-screen timing software, and royalty free audio clips.

eBook* ISBN 978-1-891440-96-0   **$9.95**

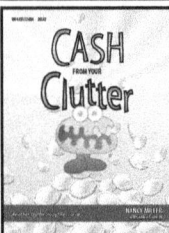

Cash From Your Clutter

A manual filled with resources to help you turn your excess stuff into cash. Includes information on what sells, where to sell your excess stuff, how to place a realistic sales value on your stuff, the best time to sell your stuff, how to donate for tax deductions, a special section on how to sell your timeshare property and much more.

Book   ISBN 978-1-891440-73-1   **$15.95**
eBook* ISBN 978-1-891440-79-3   **$9.95**

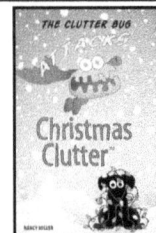

The Clutter Bug Attacks Christmas Clutter™

If there's one time of the year our homes and lives become more cluttered, it's Christmas. Here are quick and easy ways to simplify Christmas, including how to: plan and organize your Christmas, get your card and gift lists under control, simplify your gift giving, handle the gifts you receive, and get rid of Christmas clutter!

Book   ISBN 978-1-891440-74-8   **$15.95**
eBook* ISBN 978-1-891440-84-7   **$9.95**

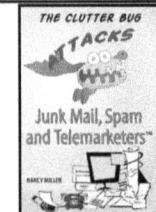

The Clutter Bug Attacks Junk Mail, Spam and Telemarketers™

Overwhelmed by Junk Mail? Spam? Telemarketers? These can all be stopped! Current, verified information with visual examples for quick and easy understanding. The first book ever to show you how to get off of political mailings, plus proven and structured processes for both eliminating and retaining communications.

eBook* ISBN 978-1-891440-81-6   **$9.95**

**eBooks contain a complete book in PDF for use on all Mac & Windows PCs, including desktops, notebooks/laptops, netbooks & tablets.*
+*All data files are in PDF format, playable/viewable on Windows and Mac, audio files are in Wave format playable on standard CD players.*

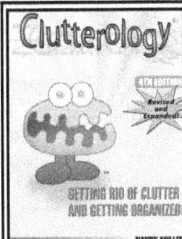

Clutterology® Getting Rid of Clutter and Getting Organized! 4th Edition

Revised and Expanded! A complete manual on how to get organized, set up and maintain manageable filing systems, and eliminate clutter that gets in your way. Provides some of the simplest, easiest and most practical advice on how to remove the clutter from your life and get organized.

Book	ISBN 978-1-891440-89-2	**$34.95**
eBook*	ISBN 978-1-891440-71-7	**$9.95**

Highlights of Clutterology®

This audio CD has over 60 minutes of tips, tricks, insights, and stories about getting rid of your clutter and getting organized. It's ideal for reinforcement to remind you that getting organized is a step-by-step process that you can accomplish if you take it easy and stick with it.

Audio CD+	ISBN 978-1-891440-44-1	**$19.95**

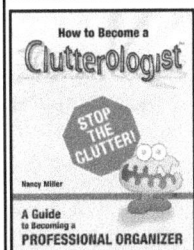

How to Become a Clutterologist™

Do label makers and shelf dividers make you smile? Use your aptitude for organization to change lives and turn your decluttering skills into a moneymaking career; become a professional organizer! Includes the tools and knowledge you need to succeed in the professional organizer industry: organizing specialties, understanding the Clutter-Hoarding Scale, how to structure your business for SUCCESS, business licensing and insurance.

Book	ISBN 978-1-891440-56-4	**$34.95**
eBook*	ISBN 978-1-891440-68-7	**$9.95**

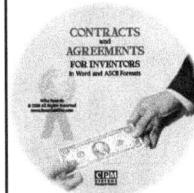

Contracts and Agreements for Inventors

Over a dozen of the most utilized agreements to help ensure that what's yours stays yours. With the help of an attorney, they contain everything you'll need from a confidentiality agreement to work-for-hire agreements, assignment of rights, and partnership agreements. Comes with instructions for usage, filling out, and filing where applicable.

Data CD+		**$19.95**

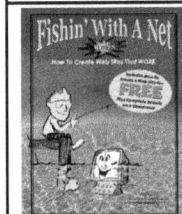

Fishin' With A Net, 10th Edition

Learn the elements of designing a Web site that actually works for you and can be created in less than four hours. Covers what the Web really is, what to put on your site to be successful, and how to link with the search engines quickly and easily.

Book	ISBN 978-1547102914	**$34.95**

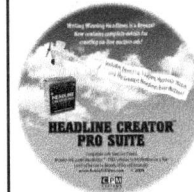

Headline Creator™ Pro Suite

"Your headline can result in 80 percent or more of the effectiveness of your ad or sales page!" Automatically generates time-tested, proven, results-oriented headlines based on the greatest headlines in history. . . and does it in 17 seconds!

Windows Software CD+		**$39.95**

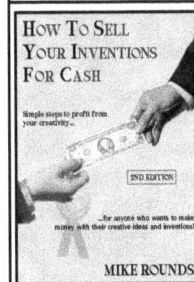

How To Sell Your Inventions for Cash, 3rd Edition

Everything you need to know to be a successful inventor! Takes your idea from inception through the licensing process to a manufacturer for royalties. Learn how to protect your inventions using patents, trademarks, copyrights, and other legal instruments, determine if you're ready to offer your idea, and how to find and solicit manufacturers who are interested in your ideas.

Book	ISBN 978-1-891440-59-5	**$24.95**
eBook*	ISBN 978-1-891440-63-2	**$9.95**
Audio CD+	ISBN 978-1-891440-28-1	**$39.95**

---

*eBooks contain a complete book in PDF for use on all Mac & Windows PCs, including desktops, notebooks/laptops, netbooks & tablets.
+All data files are in PDF format, playable/viewable on Windows and Mac, audio files are in Wave format playable on standard CD players.

Intellectual Property Protection for the Clueless®

CD contains 3 hours of audio plus 100s of pages in PDF format on trademarks, patents and copyright. Includes forms for filing without an attorney! *Bonus: How to Apply for an Innovation Research Grant!* This audio is in MP3 format playable with the Windows Media Player or comparable MP3 software.

MP3 Audio/Data CD[+]   ISBN 978-1-891440-67-0   **$59.95**

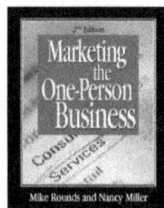

Marketing the One-Person Business, 2nd Edition

A one-person business is different from any other because you have to do the business PLUS get the business. Contains complete information about setup, operation, independent contractor criteria and forms, fee setting, consulting, public speaking, seminars, contracts and agreements.

Book   ISBN 978-1-891440-29-8   **$24.95**
eBook* ISBN 978-1-891440-88-5   **$9.95**

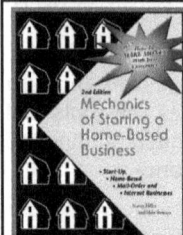

Mechanics of Starting a Home-Based Business, 2nd Edition

A home-based business is a business whose primary office is in the owner's home. Explains the realities of starting and operating a home business and including resources for taxes, licenses, and advertising plus computer operated business you can start and run.

Book   ISBN 978-1-891440-64-9   **$34.95**
eBook* ISBN 978-1-891440-70-0   **$9.95**

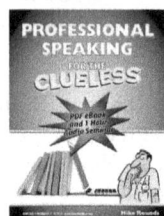

Professional Speaking for the Clueless®

Do you want to be paid to speak? This book explains the REAL business of professional speaking and how to make six figures a year without huge marketing and advertising costs. Includes dozens of resources, databases, and complete explanations of how to locate speaking opportunities and market to them.

Audio/Data CD[+]   ISBN 978-1-891440-53-3   **$24.95**
eBook*   ISBN 978-1-891440-91-5   **$9.95**

Profitable Publishing for the Clueless®

The complete 3 CD set containing everything you need to know to generate, protect, and market your printed work. See full description for each item.

Disk 1 - Self-Publishing for the Clueless®
Disk 2 - Trademarks & Copyrights for the Clueless®
Disk 3 - Book Marketing for the Clueless®

Audio/Data CD[+]   ISBN 978-1-891440-51-9   **$59.95**

Project Management for the Clueless®

Zipped file containing a 1-hour audio seminar and all of the documents you'll need to organize, plan and budget most projects in three hours or less.

Book   ISBN 978-1534869825   **$39.95**
eBook* ISBN 978-1-891440-95-3   **$9.95**

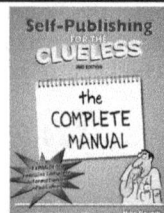

Self-Publishing for the Clueless®, 2nd Edition

Complete workbook on self-publishing, e-publishing, and a secured access to a 270 page manual with the latest information, resources, and insider tips about the world of e-publishing including how to be e-published in a week.

Workbook and Data CD[+]   ISBN 978-1-891440-99-1   **$34.95**

---

eBooks contain a complete book in PDF for use on all Mac & Windows PCs, including desktops, notebooks/laptops, netbooks & tablets.
+*All data files are in PDF format, playable/viewable on Windows and Mac, audio files are in Wave format playable on standard CD players.*

Rounds Miller
AND ASSOCIATES

Business, Technology and Organizing Training Specialists

ORDER FORM

ITEM (See Catalog for Full Description)	Format	Qty.	Price
Audio/Video Conversion Suite CD	Data CD $24.95		
Book Marketing for the Clueless®	Audio/Data CD $24.95		
	eBook - Online $9.95	PURCHASE ONLINE	
Business Training for the Clueless®	eBook - Online $9.95	PURCHASE ONLINE	
Cash From Your Clutter	Book $15.95		
	eBook - Online $9.95	PURCHASE ONLINE	
The Clutter Bug Attacks Christmas Clutter™	Book $15.95		
	eBook - Online $9.95	PURCHASE ONLINE	
The Clutter Bug Attacks Junk Mail, Spam and Telemarketers™	eBook - Online $9.95	PURCHASE ONLINE	
Clutterology® Getting Rid of Clutter and Getting Organized!	Book $34.95		
	eBook - Online $9.95	PURCHASE ONLINE	
Highlights of Clutterology®	Audio CD $19.95		
How to Become a Clutterologist™	Book $34.95		
	eBook - Online $9.95	PURCHASE ONLINE	
Contracts and Agreements for Inventors	Data CD $19.95		
Fishin' With A Net 10th Edition	Book $34.95		
Headline Creator™ Pro Suite	Software CD $39.95		
How To Sell Your Inventions for Cash	Book $24.95		
	eBook - Online $9.95	PURCHASE ONLINE	
	Audio CD $39.95		
Intellectual Property Protection for the Clueless®	MP3 Audio/Data CD $59.95		
Marketing the One-Person Business	Book $24.95		
	eBook - Online $9.95	PURCHASE ONLINE	
Mechanics of Starting a Home-Based Business	Book $34.95		
	eBook - Online $9.95	PURCHASE ONLINE	
Professional Speaking for the Clueless®	Audio/Data CD $24.95		
	eBook - Online $9.95	PURCHASE ONLINE	
Profitable Publishing for the Clueless®	3 Audio/Data CDs $59.95		
Project Management for the Clueless®	Book $39.95		
	eBook - Online $9.95	PURCHASE ONLINE	
Self-Publishing for the Clueless®	Workbook & Data CD $34.95		
Venture Capital for the Clueless®	Audio/Data CD $24.95		
	eBook - Online $9.95	PURCHASE ONLINE	
Virtual Business for the Clueless®	Book $39.95		
Whadda We Do NOW?™	Book $29.95		

Page 1 Sub-Total		

E-Books are available for
purchase and instant download online
at www.RMACart.com/E-Books.htm

Thank You!

Amount from Page 1		
Sub-Total		
in CA add Sales Tax 9.5%		
Shipping	**$2.95**	
Total		

Name (please print) _____

Mailing Address: _____

City, State, ZIP: _____

Tel: _____ e-Mail: _____

I authorize Rounds, Miller and Associates to charge my credit card for the items listed above

VISA   AMERICAN EXPRESS Cards   MasterCard   DISCOVER NOVUS

Credit Card Number: _____ exp. _____ CSS_____

Signature: _____ Date: _____

_____

To Order By Mail:

Send completed order form and check payable to Rounds, Miller and Associates to

6318 Ridgepath Court

Rancho Palos Verdes, CA 90275

View our entire product line at www.RoundsMiller.com

www.ingramcontent.com/pod-product-compliance
Lightning Source LLC
Chambersburg PA
CBHW081154090426
42736CB00017B/3319